God Sees a Beautiful You

God Sees a beautiful you

Martha Roper Saul

BROADMAN PRESS
Nashville, Tennessee

4252-67
ISBN: 0-8054-5267-2

Dewey Decimal Classification: 248.843
Subject headings: CHRISTIAN LIFE

Library of Congress Catalog Card Number: 78-72275
Printed in the United States of America

To
Glenn
Leslie, Stephen, and Susan
With love

Acknowledgments

I am grateful to various people who were helpful in the writing of this book. Those who probably deserve the bulk of the credit are the beautiful Tuesday-morning people at Southside Baptist Church, Tempe, Arizona, for whom this study was first prepared. Their warm response and encouragement meant more to me than they realized.

I am also grateful to Glenn, Carol, Rachel, Rosie, Frances, and Phyllis R. Each of them knows what he or she did to help. And thanks to Naymond who loaned me his typewriter while mine was ill.

Abbreviations and Translations

Contents

Additional Study Resources

For an in-depth study of Paul's greeting to the Roman Christians see J. W. MacGorman, *Romans: Everyman's Gospel* (Nashville; Convention Press, 1976). Out of print. See also Clifton J. Allen, *The Gospel According to Paul.* Nashville: Broadman Press, 1973 and Harper Shannon, *Riches in Romans.* Nashville: Broadman Press, 1969.

1
God Sees a Beautiful You

At twelve years of age I believed God was calling me into a Christian vocation. I felt that he at least had a job for me to do. He had tapped me on the shoulder and my reply to God was, "Yes, I am willing; here I am. Use me."

Ironically, as soon as I said yes to God, my life began to fall miserably apart. For two years it seemed that everything collapsed, and by the time I entered the ninth grade I was completely demolished. My family had moved; I couldn't seem to fit into a new school; all my friends had been left behind and so had all my confidence. I developed an overwhelming inferiority complex. Part of this was due to a physical problem, but most of it was simply the pangs of puberty. Growing up was shattering. But God soon began to put me back together, very slowly, brick-by-brick. It took years.

During this time, I experienced some of the most poignant temptations I've ever faced. I found some security in a steady boyfriend, but the problem of temptation was eternal. I was constantly battling it. Although I never gave up or gave in, neither did I win every battle. The questions that plagued me were, Why don't I behave the way I want to? Why can't I do what I know is right?

On top of the constant battle with temptation and the miserable lack of self-confidence, I was faced with a more overriding question: Who am I? (I was never sure who I was.) Was I born to be a wreck, a failure, a chronic sinner? Was I meant for better things? (It would have been such a relief to be worth something.)

I was, of course, battling the adolescent identity crisis. I was almost overwhelmed by it during those years. Sometimes, when the circumstances of my life change drastically, the same identity crisis rises up in a shadier form to haunt me once again.

All of us are faced with discovering who we are. Each of us must decide how to deal with the pressures and problems of life. And each person must conclude what kind of conduct feels right or wrong.

Sometime ago I read Karl Menninger's book, *Whatever Became of Sin?* In the epilogue he says,

> Clergymen have a golden opportunity to prevent some of the accumulated misapprehensions—guilt, aggressive action, and other roots of later mental disease.
>
> How? Preach! Tell it like it is. Say it from the pulpit. Cry it from the housetops.
>
> What shall we cry?
>
> Cry comfort, cry repentance, cry hope.[1]

The Bible does just that—it cries comfort, repentance, and hope. It did that for me.

Dr. Menninger ends his book with Socrates' haunting question, "How is it that men know what is good, but do what is bad?" What is it that causes us to make the wrong choice, to go the wrong way? These are the questions that Paul deals with in the book of Romans.

As a high school and college student I returned to the book of Romans again and again. I read it and reread it. I still return to it periodically.

I discover people today—Christians—who are wondering, "Does God really know me? Does he know who I am? Does he love me?" The book of Romans affirms that he does. It cries comfort. God truly knows you, it says, and he has plans for your life. He wants you to know yourself; he wants you to know his plans. He will help you to know both.

During times of struggle I have faced the haunting question, "How is it that I know what is good but do what is wrong?" or "How is it that I know what is good, but fail to do anything?" or "How is it that I meant to do good, but it turned out wrong?" "Why is life so frustrating?"

In Romans, Paul helps us to find answers. He not only cries repentance, he cries hope. God sees you as you really are, but he also sees you as you can be with his help.

Sin is a negative force and it messes you up; but no matter what your circumstances may be, God sees a beautiful you.

---

[1] Karl Menninger, *Whatever Became of Sin?* (New York: Hawthorn Books, Inc., 1973), p. 228.

2
Hello, You Beautiful People!

Romans 1:1-17

All of us would like to be a beautiful specimen of humanity. Some people cherish dreams of having great athletic ability; others prefer to be gorgeous and talented. Pictures of handsome executives and high-fashion models are thrown at us constantly. Opinions differ about what a beautiful person is.

We often read accounts of those who are called today's "beautiful people." Wealthy and attractive, they jet from ski resorts to the French Riviera soaking up the sun and living the good life. Today might find them in New York, tomorrow in Paris or Rome. "Ah," you may think "that's the way to live!"

Paul wrote to a group of beautiful people in Rome. It was nineteen centuries ago when there were no jet planes or ski resorts. Surprisingly, Paul himself probably never had seen these people. Yet he longed to see them, and his letter expressed warm love and appreciation for them.

These were beautiful people, not because they were wealthy or at the top of the social structure, although a few of them might have been. They were beautiful people because they were God's people. They were believers in Jesus of Nazareth. They were followers of the rugged Galilean who was crucified. They were Christians who had staked their lives on the belief that he rose in power from the grave. Not only was he still alive, his Spirit lived in them. It was the Spirit of Jesus who made them beautiful. Following him filled their lives with excitement.

Because Christianity was not a legal religion in Rome, adventure and risk were involved in living the Christian life. Paul understood what they were going through. His own experiences were similar to theirs. "You are always in my prayers. . . . I am longing to see you," he wrote (Rom. 1:9–11, Phillips). Why? "I want to bring you some spiritual gift to deepen your faith" (Rom. 1:11, Phillips).

Paul wanted to share with them some of the exciting things Christ had been doing in his life. He wanted to encourage them to "hang in there" when the going got tough. He had a word for them from the Lord.

The sharing Paul had in mind would be a mutual sharing. He wanted to give to them, but he also needed to receive from them. It would strengthen and encourage him to hear firsthand about their faith in Christ, to know how God was sustaining them, to learn about their joys and sorrows as followers of Christ. He wanted to hear their word from the Lord.

This is the kind of Christian fellowship all of us long for. We are hungry to share ourselves with those who will understand. We need the support of a loving and praying group. Jesus knew how desperately people needed to be loved and accepted. "This I command you," he said, "to love one another" (John 15:17, RSV).

Paul felt deeply indebted to these Christians at Rome. In fact, Paul felt a responsibility to all people. He recognized the worth of every single individual, regardless of background or status in life. "I owe something to all men, from cultured Greek to ignorant savage" (Rom. 1:14, Phillips). In short he had learned the secret that most of us are still groping for: how to relate meaningfully to all sorts of persons, educated and uneducated, cultured or unrefined, very rich or very poor, the well-adjusted and the maladjusted. Everyone, if you look deeply enough, is a beautiful person—made in the image of God. Everyone is worth relating to.

Then Paul penned the words that Christians have been quoting ever since. It is the word that Paul had both for the Roman Christians and also for us: "For I am not ashamed of the gospel: it is the power of God for salvation to everyone who has faith" (Rom. 1:16, RSV).

The power of God working for my salvation! The important question is: Salvation from what? Salvation from lostness—all kinds of lostness. People are lost from the beautiful life. They are lost from peace, lost from hope, lost from friendship, lost from purpose, lost from God. Each of us must ask himself the question: What do I need to be saved from? Boredom, guilt, hostility, hatred, fear, anxiety, self-centeredness? Sin?

Salvation is a process. It is better not only to say, "I am saved," but also, "I am being saved." We're saved from some of these conditions an inch at a time. But the important thing is that *the power of God is available for salvation.* We must be applying it always in our own lives.

All of us live lives that are messed up to some extent. No one's life is perfect. How is yours messed up? What do you need to be saved from? You may be facing a job loss or some big disappointment. You may be experiencing overwhelming temptation. You could be going through a change or a crisis which causes personality disorientation. Who am I? What is my purpose in life?

Some people feel these crises more keenly than others. To some they come early in life; others face them in middle years—perhaps when earlier goals of marrying, finding the right vocation, and rearing a family have already been achieved, and the future fails to look challenging. *Now* what do I want to do? Too many people wake up suddenly ro realize, "I don't like myself, my life, or my partner."

Then there are those of us who seem to spend all our time just battling the small annoyances and conflicts that arise continually within the family, on the job, in the church, or in the neighborhood. And what future is there in that—unless we have some purpose in mind, some sense of direction, some feeling of achievement?

I have not even mentioned those who battle incurable illnesses, disability, or death. Neither have I touched on the tragedies of divorce or the death of a spouse or a child.

The power of God is available—not necessarily to take us out of the situation, but certainly to see us through it, to make some kind of sense out of it, to keep us from being helpless victims. Being victimized is no fun. God's power is available to rescue us.

Perhaps you are thinking, *But Paul is speaking of power to rescue from sin. What do feelings of inferiority, loneliness, or boredom have to do with sin? And what relation do disability and death have to sinfulness?* (No, I am not about to tell you that illness comes as a punishment for sin!) But let's do examine sin in the next chapter. What is it, how do we get it, and how does it affect our lives?

Also remember Paul's words, "I see in it God's plan for making men right in his sight, a process begun and continued by their faith" (Rom. 1:17, Phillips). What does it mean to be "right" in God's sight?

We can say this much. Being right in God's sight means to believe God's love and accept it. It means to accept his plan to rescue us from lostness and offers us a meaningful purpose for living. And it means responsibility, heavy responsibility at times. Along with all of this goes a beautiful feeling—the feeling of being right with ourselves and with God.

Hello, you beautiful people!

To Do:

What do you need to be rescued from? Share the need with a small group or with a caring Christian friend. Begin to pray about your need.

3
Are You One of the Uglies?

Romans 1:18-32

I don't know anyone who wants to be ugly. But I know some handsome people who think of themselves as ugly. Often such a person will pick out a single feature—a long nose, big ears, small eyes—and feel very unattractive because of that one imperfection.

I have seen other people, impeccably groomed with beautiful features, who appear unattractive because of a sour personality.

In Romans 1:18-32, Paul describes some ugly people. They are ugly because of the way they live. These are greedy, envious, spiteful people. They gossip, lie, fight, kill, and engage in other diabolical pastimes.

Why do they live this way? you might wonder. *They must not know about God.* As a matter of fact, Paul says, they *do* know about God. They are aware of his presence through the splendor of nature. They realize God deserves their honor and praise, but they arrogantly ignore God and go their own way. Clearly these people are sinners.

How would you define sin? Perhaps you would begin by giving a list similar to the one Paul has given to describe these unbelievers. Does such a list (hating, cheating, lying, commiting adultery) explain the "disease" or merely list the symptoms?

Paul's list simply shows the result of a peoples' decision to ignore God. The people he described wasted their lives and the lives of others in shameful and appalling ways. It was not a pretty picture.

The creation story, in contrast, is a beautiful one. As it unfolds through chapter 1 of Genesis, the phrase, "and God saw that it was good," is repeated several times. After the creation of man, the account ends with a statement of great satisfaction, "and behold, it was very good" (Gen. 1:31, RSV).

God created a good world. Nothing was wrong with it. What, then, has happened to our world since the time of creation? We know the simple story of how the serpent came to Eve; we can see that since that time the world has not been so good. We are aware that people are pitifully messed up. We wish life were not so tragic. We wish people were not so mean.

Paul gives us a warning at the beginning of Romans 2. Don't shake your head and say, "Those poor sinners. They deserve God's judgment for being so awful!"

"You, who are so ready to sit in judgment on others," he says, "do the same things yourselves!" (vv. 1-2, author's paraphrase).

We are all included. We must confess, if we're honest, that Paul's list fits us, too. We have all lied, gossiped, and fought; we have all known hatred, greed, and envy. Why are we, who claim to know God, affected in the same ways as are those who refuse to know God?

In the Old Testament there are several Hebrew words for sin. One of these is the word *chatá* which simply means missing the mark. The picture is one of an archer who fails to hit the target. Often our lives are not on target; we may not necessarily intend to do wrong. We simply fail to go in the direction where God would have pointed us.

Another Hebrew word for sin is the word *pashá*, which means rebellion against God, disobedience—always intentional and deliberate. If this rebellion against God became a habit or a chosen way of life, the adjective used was *rashá* which means wicked.

Some people have the idea that sin is merely a matter of keeping or breaking the moral rules. Many believe that we please God if we observe the do's and especially the don't's; the sinners are those who break the rules. This idea has hung around because it is partly true. But, as we all know, half-truths are false.

Most of us have observed that no matter how good we try to be—no matter how hard we work at keeping the rules, we still fail to be the kind of person God expects us to be. We find that the rules, especially as Jesus interpreted them (see Matt. 5), are indeed hard to keep. This was Paul's problem (Rom. 7:15-24) and that of countless other Christians down through the ages. Even when we do not intentionally rebel *(pashá)*, we *chatá*—we fail to measure up to God's expectations.

Another concept of sin is the belief that sin has been a built-in characteristic of the human race ever since the fall of man. Some Christians believe that sin is a matter of "bad seed" passed down from Adam to all mankind, making the race inherently evil. Most non-Christian philosophers tend to agree that the human race is rather hopeless. We repeat the same mistakes over and over without any noticeable evidence of improvement.

If we believe that sin goes much deeper than merely the breaking of rules, must we then say that all human beings are born with a sinful, crooked nature? Do we inherit sin genetically from Adam? Is it passed on from parent to child in the same way that the color of our skin, the shape of our eyes, and the size of our bones were passed on to us? No, because sin, in that case, would not be our own responsibility.

Neither do we want to agree with those who say there never was a time when sin was not a part of humanity. Rather, we want to say there never was a time when mankind did not have a choice.

Isaiah said, "All we like sheep have gone astray; we have turned every one to his own way; and the Lord has laid on him the iniquity of us all" (Isa. 53:6, RSV).

This implies that although we were born innocent, all of us have departed from that innocence. We were born into a sinful world, and almost immediately we caught a weakness for sin. We learned right away to be egocentric and disobedient. Much of this we learned as a sort of "survival technique" in our messed-up world. Professor Edmond Cherbonnier put it this way:

> A newborn infant who came into the world completely without sin would still be inevitably affected by the emotional environment in which we all live—a milieu which any psychiatrist can testify is thoroughly shot through by strategies and structures of malice. From the moment of birth he becomes a victim, not of a defective human nature, but of what man has done to man. Obliged to fend for himself in such a world, he then grows up to become a party to the perpetuation of hardheartedness in his own right.[1]

Just as the serpent convinced Eve that God was not completely on the level, so we look around—whether deliberately or unconsciously—and believe there would be real advantage in choosing our own way. These choices do for us the same thing they did for Adam and Eve. Long ago our race lost the perfect harmony of environment. We also lost the perfect harmony of personal relationships. And each of us in turn becomes lost from God, lost from one another, and lost from our very own selves.

Consider a modern parable as an illustration of our human condition. Imagine with me in a kind of science-fiction context that God is the great, benevolent, all-wise, totally good doctor of science who creates a marvelous little world of people. It is a beautiful world with flowers, grass, trees, streams, animals, and perfect little people. They are people who know only perfect health, extravagant happiness, and loving relationships. They take care of their world, its animals, and they take care of one another.

The creative doctor knows each little person by name and delights in the individuality of each one. Each of the creatures derives happiness not only from being busily creative in his own way but also from knowing the good doctor personally and being able to please him and respond to his kindness.

All goes well until an enemy sneaks into the doctor's laboratory, bringing to the little world a foreign germ. The people know they should accept only that which comes from the hand of their father-doctor, but some of them are beguiled by the enemy into disobeying and out of curiosity they accept what the enemy has brought.

The germ begins to wreak havoc in the once-perfect little world. The people who are infected no longer act normal, and right away it becomes evident that they are ill. The infection spreads; soon even the animals and the total environment are affected. The whole world becomes very much out of order. It begins to die.

In their sickness, the people are beguiled. They suffer delusions which are pleasurable. Most of them know they are sick, but they hang onto the pleasure in their sickness. Some refuse to admit they're sick at all.

The sad doctor, at monumental personal sacrifice and expense, manages to develop an antitoxin to combat the effects of the enemy's germ. Those who take the antitoxin will eventually be completely well, good as new, although their progress may be slow and sometimes unsteady. The saddest part of the story is that some of the people refuse to take the cure. They prefer the disease, or they stubbornly refuse to admit they need help.

The good doctor will eventually have to evaluate the condition of each person to determine who has taken the antitoxin and is in the process of recovering, and who has refused any help. Those who refuse will, for obvious reasons, have to be removed. But will the little world ever be the same again?

The Bible gives us the answer: There will eventually be a new heaven and a new earth.

In the meantime, how is your own cure progressing? Do you recognize sin in your own life and in your world? What are you doing to help yourself and those around you until the time comes when everything will be perfect again?

[1] E. La B. Cherbonnier, *Hardness of Heart: A Contemporary Interpretation of the Doctrine of Sin* (Naperville, Ill.: Allenson, 1955), p. 136.

To Think About:

1. What traces of ugliness (sin) do you see in your own spiritual mirror? Recognize the fact that sin is not an original part of your nature. It is not the "real" you. Decide to deal honestly with it in your life.

2. One way to deal with sin is to "call it as you see it." Recognize *hatred* and call it that. Face up to *gossiping.* Call *lying* by its true name. This is a part of learning—to be responsible for our own lives.

4
Who's OK?

Romans 2 and 3

I'm OK, You're OK has been a popular book for several years. The author, Thomas Harris, explains how most of us see other people as being basically OK, but we feel that we ourselves do not measure up. According to the writer, most of us grew up with negative feelings about ourselves because we were continually "put down" by our parents and others who were important to us.

We recognize the truth in what he said. All of us long to be persons who really are OK. We want to feel good about who we are and how we do things. We want to feel good about what we're accomplishing in life. We need to feel worthwhile to ourselves and to other people.

People who think deeply, though realize that they actually are not living up to their own potential. Most of us recognize that we do fall short of what we would like to be and what we sense we were created to be.

Too often we attempt to deal with the problem by "putting down" the people around us. If we can convince ourselves that others aren't doing so well, then we feel better in comparison. We do the same thing to them that was done to us. We devalue them. Sometimes we do it only silently, within ourselves.

One way to devalue others is by judging their actions or their morality. Paul reminds us in Romans 2 that we are quick to condemn others for the same things we do ourselves. "Therefore you have no excuse . . . whoever you are, when you judge another; for in passing judgment upon him you condemn yourself, because you, the judge, are doing the very same things" (Rom. 2:1, RSV). Jesus, too, talked about people who go after a speck in someone else's eye while ignoring the beam in their own eye (Matt. 7:3).

The universal tendency for people to knock others down in order to prop themselves up is a deception as old as Adam and Eve. When Adam was ashamed to face God, he blamed Eve for his situation. He even blamed God for giving him Eve in the first place. Adam was deeply hurt and disappointed—in himself. He was looking for someone, anyone, to take the responsibility from his shoulders.

The habit of judging other people harshly and shifting the blame to someone else for our own shortcomings is a violation of truth. It's a refusal to face the truth about ourselves. It's a refusal to bring our lives into line with God's truth. You probably noticed that Paul speaks rather strongly in the last part of chapter 1 and throughout chapter 2 about God's judgment of those who live contrary to the truth (see Rom. 1:18; 2:8). God naturally cannot condone a way of life that so completely wrecks the people he loves and the world they live in. How could he be neutral about such a situation?

You will notice that for now his judgment consists largely in his finally agreeing to "give people up," allowing them to go their own way (see Rom. 1:24,26,28).

The worst thing that can happen to us is for God to allow us to go our own way, but he will permit us if we insist.

In Romans 3:10-18 Paul evaluates the human race in a sad but scathing collection of Old Testament quotations. He begins this way: "None is righteous, no, not one; no one understands, no one seeks for God. All have turned aside, together they have gone wrong; no one does good, not even one" (vv. 10-12, RSV).

This is not an attempt to further destroy our already sagging self-esteem. Rather, it is a plea for honesty.

God is seeking our fellowship, just as he went seeking the fellowship of Adam and Eve in the garden twilight. But "no one understands, no one seeks for God. All have turned aside." We have become preoccupied with trying to justify ourselves. Like Adam and Eve we hide from the truth, and when we finally show up, we are covered with fig leaves—that is, we are covered up with whatever act might make us look better.

God wants us to stand before him honestly: "Yes, God, I lied today. Yes, I fought with everyone around me. Yes, I did kill someone with a few choice words. Yes, I am envious of someone else's accomplishments. I recognize that I'm falling short, and I want to do better."

When we're willing to face him honestly, to stand before him without subterfuge, God can relate to us again as he wants to. He can enter again into our lives and begin to show us how to deal with the problem in a truly constructive way. That is the most important step toward solving our problem of inner failure.

We may be stuck with the desire to look good to other people. How are we to deal with that? Part of the answer lies in recognizing that others are facing the same situation that we face. Their lives are not perfect either. They, too, are struggling with failure in one area or another. Paul says "there is no distinction; since all have sinned and fall short of the glory of God" (Rom. 3:22-23, RSV). Or as Phillips translates it, "Everyone has sinned, everyone falls short of the beauty of God's plan."

Some people may appear to be doing better with their lives than you are. The tendency is to feel that those people are worth more than you. On the other hand, there are lives that look worse than yours. They may even be worse in the sense that their actions are more harmful or more destructive. Basically, though, we're all in the same boat. No one measures up to his full potential. Everyone is hindered from being all that he wants to be.

But we can quit playing the games that alienate us from ourselves, from other people, and from God. Those are the games of always critically evaluating others, blaming someone else for our own shortcomings, and denying the truth about ourselves. We are fully human when we face God and face the world as we really are—without shame and without cover-up. Being OK in the deepest sense means being righteous, being fully committed to the truth. Jesus said, "I am the truth" (John 14:6). He who created us and loves us also pronounces us OK when we give ourselves to him.

To Think About:

1. Do you avoid God when you feel that you haven't measured up? Or do you seek him, believing God will

come to you in a fair and loving way, ready to make you OK again?

2. "Everyone falls short of the beauty of God's plan" (Rom. 3:23, Phillips). Have you discovered God's beautiful plan for your life? Are you "missing the mark," or are you discovering the beautiful you that God had in mind?

3. There was a problem of prejudice in the church at Rome. The Jewish Christians felt that they were better than the Gentile Christians. Notice how Paul dealt with the problem in chapters 2 and 3 by affirming the worth of both groups.

5

Take Your Cue from Father Abe
. . . He Was A-OK

Romans 4

What does it take to be friends with God? What makes us OK in his sight? Abraham serves as Paul's great example of a person who was OK with God. " 'Abraham believed God and it was credited to him as righteousness,' and he was called God's friend" (Jas. 2:23, NIV).

Twice in the fourth chapter of Romans Paul repeats the Old Testament statement: "Abraham believed God and it was credited to him as righteousness" (Rom. 4:3,22). *Abraham believed God.* That's the reason he was OK in his relationship with God.

Like human friendships, friendship with God is based not on rule-keeping but on responsiveness and trust. Adam's relationship with God was that way in the beginning. He trusted God; he followed God's instructions.

One of the first things God told Abraham was that he should go completely away from his heathen nation; he should pick up his wife and belongings and go off to an unknown land to see what kind of plans God had for him—and God had astonishing plans for him! He was entering into partnership with God.

Here is what God said to Abraham: "Go from your country and your kindred . . . to the land that I will show you. And I will make of you a great nation, and I will bless you and make your name great, so that you will be a blessing" (Gen. 12:1-2, RSV).

We might paraphrase Abraham's "call" like this: "Come out of the place where you're living, and I will show you where to go." The call is somewhat the same for us today. Psychologists are telling us more and more insistently that our kingdoms are within us, that we "live where we choose to live." Although we are to a great extent products of our early environments (that is, we learn our responses to life in infancy and early childhood), yet we have the ability to change, to be what we want to be, to live where we want to live. We don't have to live with old defeats. God's power is available for us to live in new territory. With his help we can do something about our circumstances.

Those of us who are Christians heeded God's call to come out of the "old land" when we became his followers. Too many of us though have forgotten the second clause of that call: "and I will show you where to go." We sometimes come out of our "old land" with great joy but soon find ourselves beset with the same old problems. So we either "throw in the Christian towel," or we settle down for a Christian life that bears little resemblance to what it could be. We do not allow God to show us where to go. In a moment we will deal more with where God wants us to go, but for right now, let's remind ourselves of the promise that accompanied God's call to Abraham.

This was the promise to Abraham: "I will bless you . . . so that you will be a blessing" (Gen. 12:2 RSV). The promise is the same for us today: "I will bless you so that you will be a blessing."

The implication here is that God's blessing comes as we follow his directions, as we go where he shows us to go. He blesses us, as he did Abraham, because he loves us and so that we can be a blessing to other people. The really happy, the really healthy (in Spirit), really beautiful people on this earth are those who are giving happiness to other people because they are being blessed by God. They are going into territory that God has shown them.

Do not assume that you found God's will long ago, and so you are set for life—or that you missed it long ago and that was that. Gail Sheehy's book, *Passages*, points out that as adults we go through various stages of growth. Each stage calls for choices that are crucial. Having chosen a vocation or a life-style once, you should not assume that you are done with choosing. God may have a new place for you to go.

The great commitment of each life should be to God's will, and God has new plans for new years. He has new revelations and fresh insight always ready for us—whenever we are ready. There are times in life when it is imperative that we broaden our experiences, that we change our outlook, that we re-evaluate goals, that we take a new direction. Otherwise we face stagnation.

How do you know whether God is leading you into some new venture, as he did Abraham? How do you know when God is calling you to be more than you ever dreamed of being?

Sometimes it is fun to brainstorm about the future. (Do this alone or with a partner.) What is the most exciting thing you can think of doing? What have you always wanted to do that seemed out of reach for you? What abilities do you have that never have been fully utilized? Should you return to school? Should you develop a particular talent—music, art, drama? Should you get special training? Try a business venture? Could you give some years to a mission assignment? What can you do that will honestly bless other people?

Analyze your natural abilities or have them analyzed. Many universities offer free vocational and aptitude testing. Some do personality inventories. All these can be tools for understanding yourself better. They may help you to find God's will.

The soundest advice I can offer is that in all this seeking, seek God first. You have probably heard the proverb: "Happiness is a direction, not a place." I would add that happiness is, first of all, knowing God and through him knowing yourself. The psalmist said it long ago: "As a hart longs for flowing streams, so longs my soul for thee, O God"(Ps. 42:1, RSV).

It is finally and ultimately friendship with God that we long for. Peace comes from the one who said, "Peace, be still," and, "My peace I leave with you." It may not come from making some dramatic move. It comes from knowing God, from responding to his touch in your life.

In Abraham's life it was, first of all, the *believing* rather than the *going* that made the difference. He trusted what God told him. The most astounding promise of God to Abraham was that he (Abraham) would be the father of many nations; his offspring would be as numerous as the dust of the earth and the stars of the sky. But Abraham was already an old man when God *gave* him that promise, and Sarah his wife had never been able to have children. By this time she was hopelessly beyond the age of bearing children. Romans 4:20-22 says: "Yet he [Abraham] did not waver through unbelief regarding the promise of God, but was

strengthened in his faith and gave glory to God, being
fully persuaded that God had power to do what he had
promised. This is why 'it was credited to him as righteousness' " (NIV).

Abraham was chosen by God to hold a unique place
in history. He believed God, and then he acted. He is,
as Paul said, the father of all of us who place our trust
in God.

How do you place your trust in God? Consider these
questions in summary:

1. God's promises to you: What are they? Do you
believe them? The Bible is rich in promises. Some of
them should not be taken out of context. Too often
our problem is not that we misuse them, but that we
fail to use them at all. There are times in our Christian
experience when we have a deep, comforting assurance,
as Abraham did, that God has made us a promise. It
is uniquely our own; we can count on it.

2. Where does God want you to go with your life?
He may want you to stay geographically where you
are, but within our inner selves God never wants us
to remain where we are. We must grow and expand.
In our actions and activities God does not want us to
remain where we are. He wants to be our partner. He
wants to lead us in new and exciting directions.

3. What can you do that will lead to the happiness
and well-being of other people? How can you bless others? This is an important question to consider in terms
of long-range planning—choosing a vocation, an avoca-
tion, a retirement plan, an area of church or community
service. It is also a good question to ask on a daily
basis. There are many small ways in which we can give
happiness to others, but the most important of these

result from God's instruction in our lives. He shows us what to do.

Human friendships are based on responsiveness and trust. So is our friendship with God. Do you believe what God tells you and do you act on that belief? Then you, like Abraham, are OK with God.

6
You Glorious Creature!

Romans 5:1-5

Are you getting any glory out of life? If you aren't, you should be. You need it, you deserve it, and you should see that you get it! All of us fare better with some applause for being who we are and doing what we're doing!

The need for approval is one of the basic emotional needs of humans. The child who develops emotional security is the one who receives ample love and approval from people who are important to him. No matter how sophisticated we become, we do not outgrow the desire to be praised.

Many people desperately want approval, but they seek it in the wrong way. They seek it by trying to please the people they know. This is normal and healthy for children, but it seldom works for adults. The approval-seeking adult frequently ends up being a doormat for everyone who wants to walk over him.

Maurice E. Wagner in his book, *The Sensation of Being Somebody*, says most of us want to know three things concerning our function in life: How do I look? How am I doing? How important am I? We want reassurance in these areas of appearance, performance, and status.

But people who continually ask these questions

(whether verbally or nonverbally) usually get confusing answers. We simply cannot please everyone around us. And the person who approves of us today may disapprove tomorrow.

Most of us need a more stable kind of approval. We should have the kind of assurance that brings self-approval rather than a superficial pat-on-the-back from acquaintances. We're searching for a deeper and more genuine kind of glory.

Romans 5:2 says, "We rejoice in our hope of sharing the glory of God"(RSV). In the last chapter we talked about the promises of God. Throughout the Bible, glory is promised to those who please God. Usually we shrug that off as a pie-in-the-sky kind of promise. We're not sure what the promise means, but it sounds too holy to be practical.

Actually the word *glory* in the Bible means praise, esteem, approval—as it does today when we give glory to national heroes, sports figures, and prominent people. The New Testament word *doxa*, from which we get our word *doxology*, means glory or praise.

Throughout the Bible, the word *glory* was used in another significant way. It meant the visible sign of God's presence on earth. Sometimes God's presence was exhibited as an aura of brightness that struck fear or brought comfort to the beholder. It said, "God is here!" God's glory was sometimes described as a bright cloud that filled the tabernacle or Temple (see Ezek. 10:4, for example). God's glorious presence in the Exodus was evidenced by a pillar of cloud by day and a pillar of fire at night. Moses' glowing face reflected the glory of God after he had been in God's presence on the mountain (Ex. 34:29-30).

When Paul says, "We rejoice in our hope of sharing the glory of God," he is speaking of the divine splendor to be ours in the next world, but he means more than that. There are many verses in his writings and throughout the Bible which let us know that God is eager to share his glory with us right now. He wants to be the radiant presence in our lives. He wants to give the approval we're longing for.

Notice that I am using *glory* in three ways: (1) praise, esteem, approval; (2) the presence of God himself; and (3) the glow, the radiance that accompanies either of these conditions, whether it is actually seen or merely felt by the persons involved.

I am going further to suggest that God's presence indicates his attention or his approval in a person's life or in a situation. In other words, when God's purpose is being carried out, he makes his presence known. He gives his approval by being there.

This is the approval we're seeking—God's glory, which he shares with us when our lives are pleasing to him. How do we please him?

1. We please him first of all by giving glory (praise) to him, both in the words we speak and in the way we live for him.

2. We please him when his Spirit is living forcefully in our lives.

3. We please him when we are obedient to his word and to his leadership.

4. We please him when we endure trouble patiently for his sake.

Jesus exhibited more of God's glory than any other person who ever lived on earth. John wrote, "We beheld his glory, the glory of the only begotten of the Father, full of grace and truth" (John 1:14, KJV). At one point the glory of God completely transfigured him. Even his clothes became radiant. This was one of the times when God spoke his approval in an audible voice: "This is my beloved Son, with whom I am well pleased; listen to him" (Matt. 17:5; 3:17, RSV).

Jesus was completely obedient to God. He was not interested in the kind of glory that people often seek from one another. He lived only to glorify God, and he wanted for himself only the glory that God gives. He did not constantly spout "holy talk" or act more pious than other people. He was simply committed completely to doing his Father's will. He said, "I and the Father are one" (John 10:30, RSV).

Jesus dealt early in his ministry with the temptation to seek earthly glory. He turned down the temptation to be powerful or spectacular (Matt. 4:5-10). He scorned the game of collecting laurels. At one point he said to the Pharisees, "How can you believe, who receive glory from one another and do not seek the glory that comes from the only God?" (John 5:44, RSV).

Jesus' life was climaxed by suffering. Although he prayed earnestly to avoid it, he accepted the suffering obediently when the time came because it was necessary. His sole purpose was still to glorify his Father. "Now is my soul troubled. And what shall I say? 'Father, save me from this hour'? No, for this purpose I have come to this hour. Father, glorify thy name" (John 12:27-28 RSV).

You see, even trouble can be a glorious experience. It was true in Jesus' life, and it should be true in our own lives. Trouble is never going to be any fun, and something is certainly wrong if we enjoy suffering. But we can rejoice during the time of suffering because of what the outcome will be. Paul says, "And we rejoice in our troubles, because we know that trouble produces endurance, endurance brings God's approval, and his approval creates hope. This hope does not disappoint us" (Rom. 5:3-5, TEV).

"Endurance brings God's approval, and his approval creates hope!" Here it is—the approval of God. It puts a glow of confidence into the Christian life. It brings peace. Even suffering, for the Christian, results in glory.

Perhaps I have given the impression that God's approval comes to us only in mystical ways; sometimes it does. Most of us know from experience that God's approval often comes to us through other people. It comes unexpectedly and overwhelmingly from a person, but we know immediately it is God's grace. We did not ask for it or work for it. It came out of our friendship with God. It is simply the word of encouragement.

Most of us also know the warm experience of giving approval to someone else. That too comes out of our friendship with God, and it's a reminder that in the area of approval, "It is more blessed to give than to receive." I want to assure you that although approval-seeking is a misdirected activity, sincere approval-giving is of great benefit—to both giver and receiver.

Consider the following thoughts about glory:

1. "Christ is in you, which means that you will share the glory of God" (Col. 1:27, TEV).

2. "For I reckon that the sufferings of this present time are not worthy to be compared with the glory which shall be revealed in us" (Rom. 8:18, KJV).

3. "For this slight momentary affliction is preparing for us an eternal weight of glory beyond all

comparison" (2 Cor. 4:17, RSV).

4. "Rather be glad that you are sharing Christ's sufferings, so that you may be full of joy when his glory
is revealed. Happy are you if you are insulted because
you are Christ's followers; this means that the glorious
Spirit, the Spirit of God, is resting on you" (1 Pet. 4:13-
14, TEV).

5. "And we all, with unveiled face, beholding the glory
of the Lord, are being changed into his likeness from
one degree of glory to another; for this comes from
the Lord" (2 Cor. 3:18, RSV).

6. "What is man that thou art mindful of him, and
the son of man that thou dost care for him? Yet thou
hast made him little less than God, and dost crown him
with glory and honor" (Ps. 8:4-5, RSV).

Seeking God's glory is a "heavy" goal. We do not
start on this path without counting the cost. It means
shouldering obedience and responsibility, and it promises some degree of suffering. But it is the goal we
were created for. We find that when we walk this way
with Jesus, our "yoke becomes easy and our burden
light." We behold his glory and we become more like
him. We are being transformed into the glorious creatures we were meant to be.

"We confidently and joyfully look forward to becoming all that God has had in mind for us to be" (Rom.
5:2, TLB).

To Think About:

1. Are you generous in giving your approval to other
people? "Give and it shall be given to you" often applies

here. (But don't expect the same person you approve of to give you approval in return; that's tantamount to approval-seeking!)

2. Do you feel that God approves or disapproves of your life? How does he show his approval?

3. Is there any difference between seeking God's glory and seeking his will?

To Do:

For greater understanding of the concept of glory, read:

C. S. Lewis, *The Weight of Glory* (Grand Rapids: Wm. B. Eerdmans Publishing Company, 1965).

T. B. Maston, *Why Live the Christian Life?* Chapter 5, "Its Highest Motive: Glory of God" (Nashville: Thomas Nelson, Inc., 1974).

Bernard Ramm, *Them He Glorified* (Grand Rapids: Wm. B. Eerdmans Publishing Company, 1963).

7
God's Great Positive Stroke

Romans 5:5-11

A friend gave me the delightful little book, *Fuzzies*, by Richard Lessor. It's a folk fable about people whose happiness came from giving and receiving warm lovable little creatures called "Fuzzies."

Many of you are familiar with the term, "warm fuzzies." A warm fuzzie is the same thing as a positive stroke. A positive stroke is anything which someone else does that lets you know you are a person of worth. It is anything that gives you a warm, happy feeling. A positive stroke can be a pat on the shoulder, a friendly hello, a straightforward compliment, a hug, or a kiss. It can be a gift or a helpful deed or a vote of confidence. It can be an invitation or a thank-you.

The best kind of positive stroke is unconditional love—love that is based not on our looks or our actions, but on our worth as human beings. One of the most important things we needed as infants and children was unconditional love—the kind of love that continued to love us no matter what.

It's the thing we grown-ups still long for. We carry around within us the child we once were. The childhood delight and joy is there, and if we are happy, free individuals, it bubbles forth in joyful experiences still. The scars of childhood hurts remain there. In some people they've never healed, but continue to fester and cause pain and unhappiness. The security given by love or the insecurity caused by lack of love remains with us. We're only the child we were, grown up.

Jesus said, "Unless you . . . become like children, you will never enter the kingdom of heaven" (Matt. 18:3, RSV). It's a reminder that we need to affirm the child within us. God affirms that child, and he wants us to relate to him as a child relates to a loving parent. It's the only way he can do for us all that needs to be done. He wants to kiss the hurts, forgive the mistakes, quiet the fears, and teach us to laugh again.

So there is God, offering us the unconditional love we've always needed. Romans 5:5 says, "God's love has been poured into our hearts through the Holy Spirit" (RSV). It's a positive stroke to which we can sincerely reply, "Thanks, Lord. I needed that!"

Paul illuminates the unconditional nature of God's love in Romans 5:6-11 as he talks about Christ dying for us. He says Christ died for us "while we were yet helpless" (v. 6), "while we were sinners" (v. 8), and "while we were enemies" (v. 10, RSV).

It is touching and surprising, but not unheard of, to find a person willing to give up his own life for someone who is weak or helpless. Although not many people would make such a sacrifice, a few would. Occasionally we hear of someone risking his own life to save a drowning person or to save a victim of fire.

Most of us at least experience a great feeling of sympathy, even empathy, for a person who is helpless—especially for a helpless child. We would like to be able to help. Many parents would gladly give up their own lives if necessary to save the life of their child. God did that.

We were weak and helpless victims of sin when Christ died for us. It was God, sacrificing his own life for a helpless child, the victim of a terminal situation. He did it out of love.

It's quite a different matter to think of sacrificing a good life for a person who is ungodly and rebellious. Paul says a few people might agree to die for a really good person, but to die for an ungodly sinner is unheard of—yet that is what Jesus did. Unconditional love is not withdrawn when the loved one turns out to be a big disappointment.

I'm sure you've known parents whose children turned out to be painful disappointments. They were children who were intelligent, talented, and promising youngsters; yet they rejected their parents' values, and, as they grew up, went another way. They chose a lifestyle that was irresponsible or destructive. They contributed hurt and harm to the world when their parents hoped they would lend healing and help. To have rebellious and destructive children is a blow to parents, but many of them continue to offer love, help, and forgiveness.

We were God's rebellious and disappointing children, ruined by sin. But Paul says, "God shows his love for us in that while we were yet sinners Christ died for us" (Rom. 5:8, RSV).

Paul then makes a third "while-we-were" statement, and the descriptive word he uses is "enemies." Maybe you wouldn't do anything to harm an enemy of yours; hopefully you would even be willing to help such a person. But I certainly wouldn't expect you to give up your life for an enemy.

Occasionally, however, a loved one becomes an enemy. That's the situation King David faced with his son Absalom. Absalom cunningly worked to woo the allegiance of the Israelites away from his father David. After a while many of them began to love Absalom more than they loved his father. Then Absalom ruthlessly plotted a conspiracy and incited a rebellion against David so he could be king in his father's place. He and his followers even planned the death of David and the overthrow of David's army.

Things did not work out as the wicked son Absalom had planned. His army was defeated by David's men, and even though David had instructed his men to be kind to Absalom, he was mercilessly killed by David's captain.

Two messengers ran to give David the news of the battle. "It is good news," they said. "Your enemy is defeated!"

"But is Absalom all right?" David asked.

Then David had to be told that Absalom was dead. The "good news" was not good news to David. He did not want to lose his son. His grief is described in 2 Samuel 18:33: "And the king was deeply moved, and went up to the chamber over the gate, and wept; and as he went, he said, 'O my son Absalom, my son, my son Absalom! Would I had died instead of you, O Absalom, my son, my son!' " (RSV).

David would gladly have died instead of Absalom, his enemy, because his enemy was his child. Christ did for us what David could not do for his son Absalom.

He died instead of us, and his death reconciled us to God. We are no longer enemies, but beloved children of God. This answers forever the question, "Am I really loved?"

It's unfortunate how many people grow up in the church hearing over and over of God's love but never really feeling or believing it in a personal way. Somehow the reality of that love never dawns on them. How can we experience the warmth of God's love?

One way is by making it a habit to "cuddle up" to God each day. He will speak to you from the Bible; you can speak to him from your heart. Tell him what you're feeling, ask his help for the day. Thank him for his love. Express your love for him. The Holy Spirit will "pour his love into your heart."

To Think About:

1. Do you have a regular time alone with God? It can well be the most rewarding minutes of the day.

2. Sometimes it's hard to love other "sinners." It's especially hard to love our enemies. Should we refuse to do for others what God has done for us?

8
The Sweet Taste of Freedom

Romans 6 and 7

We rebel at the thought of being slaves. Yet most of us admit to being slaves to one degree or another. Some of us are slaves to our job, others to our house, to our children, to husband or wife, to a habit, to a fear, to an illness.

We may wonder, is there any such thing as freedom? Yes! We were created for freedom, not for slavery. As human beings we have a choice.

In Romans 6:16 Paul says, "You *belong* to the power which you choose to obey, whether you choose sin . . . or God . . ." (Phillips). You can choose your master. God is the Master who sets us free. Sin is the master that enslaves.

In the first three chapters of Romans we talked about sin. We're going to talk about sin again—because Paul will not let us forget that the basic human struggle is with sin.

Let's remind ourselves of the kind of master sin may be. You remember that one of the Hebrew words for sin was a hunting term which means "missing the mark." Sometimes the same word was used to mean "missing the path"—taking the wrong road. Sin might simply be defined as "failure." We might say it is failing to aim accurately with our lives or failing to take the right path in life. It involves failure to make the right choices day by day. It is failure to be what we were created to be.

Another dimension of sin, as you recall, is that of rebellion against God. Some people deliberately choose to go astray. They decide not to follow God's plan. They refuse to be what they were created to be. John Claypool says this was the basic sin of the prodigal son. He had an identity problem. He refused to be his father's son. He did not recognize his limits or his true place in the order of things. [1] In his case, sin was not just the *failure* to be what he should have been, but the *refusal* to be what he should have been.

According to the Bible, a person is responsible for all his own actions. He is accountable even for his mistakes and inaccuracies. This idea of being responsible for our own lives, for our actions, is a healthy one. It affirms that God created us as creatures of dignity, capable of choosing for ourselves.

Not many people make a conscious choice to be a failure in this life. Not many choose to be slaves to sin. Yet, there are too many people who are all bound up in one way or another. They cannot be what they would like to be. They are bound to duties and situations they do not like. They are hindered by weakness and by evil.

If thousands of people are slaves to sin, failure, and disillusionment, and if these people did not consciously choose that kind of slavery, how then can it be avoided? How can I avoid that very predicament?

The first step is simply in recognizing sin for what it is—failing to follow God's way or refusing to follow God's way.

The second step is to be aware that sin is the force of the enemy in our lives. The enemy may be quite subtle or very powerful. He works to overthrow us at whatever point we're weakest or most likely to be off-guard. He may tug us gently in the wrong direction, or he may pull us overwhelmingly the wrong way. If we do not recognize that he's there, so much the easier for him.

The third step is to keep in touch with God. Remember that his way is the way of freedom; consciously choose his way. God himself is completely free. He acts in power and in truth. He acts in love and in mercy. He is the great liberator. He shows us the way of freedom. If your life is all tied up, God is the one who can set you free.

Some forms of bondage (physical disability, for example) have to be endured until God's time to release us—even if it never comes in this life. (Remember the promise of glory to those who suffer.) But no matter what your physical restrictions may be, there is freedom for the spirit. The Christian should have a keen and exhilarating sense of freedom. I hope that you exult in that sense of freedom, no matter what your restrictions may be.

Our freedom as Christians rests on hope. Jacques Ellul makes a strong point of this in his book, *The Ethics of Freedom*. Christian hope involves much more than optimism or wishful thinking. Christian hope grows out of what God has already done for his people (the choosing of a nation, the plan of redemption, the resurrection of Jesus, for example); it looks forward to what he has promised to do at the end of the age. Our hope is the strong certainty that God will do for us all that needs to be done. That hope frees us from depression, from despair, from aimlessness. It sets our spirits on the course of joy and expectation. Good things are up ahead! I am free to participate and to enjoy all that the future holds.

Sin binds us to selfish and short-sighted pursuits. We become entangled in futile activities and pointless spending of time and money. We accept responsibilities that are drudgery; they keep us from doing the fulfilling things that are God's will for us. We get into commitments and relationships that are damaging because they involve deceit. They violate our commitment to God.

Some people think Christian commitment is bondage. They believe it takes away the freedom to do what they want to do. Their thinking may be based partly on Paul's statements that he is a slave of Jesus Christ. They rebel at the idea of being a slave—even to Jesus.

But that is one of the paradoxes of the Christian faith. The more totally obedient we are to Christ, the more completely free we are as individuals.

Jesus lived in complete freedom. He walked free of tradition, free of the opinions of other people, free of the Jewish law, free of the laws of nature. He walked free of sin. His freedom was complete only because he was completely obedient to God. He chose to follow God's will. He chose to be a servant. He chose to die. But he was raised again in power and in splendor— because that was God's way.

Let me share a personal experience which may illustrate Christian freedom. When I became pregnant with my third child, my husband and I had made a definite decision to restrict our family to two children. We thought we had met the necessary conditions to carry out that decision. You can imagine our dismay. My own reaction was rebellion. I rebelled against not being able to control my own destiny. I resented giving any more years to diapers and feedings. I resented being bound again to a baby when I wanted to be doing things with the children I already had. I resented being bound again to a schedule at home when there were exciting things to do in the church and in the world. I resented bringing another mouth into the world to feed when children were starving in other places.

As a Christian I was free to consider the alternatives. I did not have to have the baby. My doctor could arrange an abortion. (That may sound like an odious crime to you, but it is a choice in our world.) The choice was mine.

I wanted to make my decision under God. I did not actually want the responsibility of terminating a life. I did not have the wisdom or knowledge for making such a decision. God alone is Lord of life and death. I chose to wait for him.

I brought another healthy baby into the world. (She is a beautiful, intelligent, loving child who is now, of course, one of the joys of our life!) I did it in complete freedom because I did it in hope. My hope was sure and certain that God would do everything for us that needed to be done. I was sure that God could use another child in his kingdom. There was plenty of food at our house and plenty of love (not to mention the noise!). I could rejoice in having another baby because I had chosen to do so. The sacrifices were still there, but so was the presence of God. The sacrifices were there, but I had chosen to make them. It was the difference between freedom and slavery.

In his book *Them He Glorified,* Bernard Ramm lists five freedoms which the Christian finds in Christ. [2] Let me list them for you with my own comments:

1. **Freedom from sin.** Dr. Ramm explains that freedom from sin does not mean freedom from temptation, nor does it mean we will never sin again. Instead it means we are free from the *compulsion* to sin. We do not have to sin. We can choose not to sin.

2. **Freedom from the deception of sin.** Life in sin is a deception and a lie. Professor Ramm gives Paul as an example of this. Before his conversion, Paul was deceived into thinking he was righteous. He was convinced that his life was faultless and that he was truly serving God. But when he found Christ, he found freedom from deception. He also found himself, because he had found the way of truth.

3. **Freedom from the law.** When we believe that we can make ourselves good by keeping rules, we are enslaved to a false method of salvation. Paul says God's law is holy, just, and good, but it is commandment and not gospel. We cannot keep God's law, and when we break it, we have to bear the load of guilt.

Some people live under the law of "what other people think." Others live under the law of "what's expected." There are those who try to earn their salvation by being slaves to the church. Christ frees us from all the tiresome duties of earning our salvation. We live, instead, under the perfect law of freedom.

4. **Freedom from idolatry and world systems.** Paul was talking about pagan idolatry and superstitions and human regulations and philosophies. I believe this applies strongly to the popular life-styles and philoso-

phies of our day. Even some Christians are looking for freedom by trying new philosophies and new religions. Others are caught up in the ultramaterialism of our day—constant going, buying, and spending. There is great relief in the simple rule of putting God's kingdom first and letting him add the extra zip to life.

5. **Freedom from death.** Although Christians must still experience death, we do not experience its sting (the Greek word is *kentron,* the poisonous, deadly sting of the insect). We are beyond the threat and terror of dying because Jesus has done our dying for us. We can face it with confidence and hope.

Even though Christ has made us free, sin continues to exert a strong pull on our lives. Paul says that recognizing sin for what it is makes us more responsible for it and more susceptible to it (see Rom. 7:7-8). Sometimes it seems overwhelming, and we find ourselves crying out as Paul did in Romans 7:15-25, "I want to do the right thing, but the harder I try to do right, the more I do wrong!" (author's paraphrase). This is not the cry of rebellion, but the cry of failure. Some Christians give up in despair.

What can we do? Remember that Christ has set us free. It is in his will that we live in freedom (see Gal. 5:1,13). Make a deliberate choice to live the free life in Christ. And what if we find ourselves powerless to live out our choice? Don't despair, Paul says; help is available from Jesus Christ our Lord (Rom. 7:25*a*). In chapter 8 of Romans, Paul talks about the powerful help which the Holy Spirit brings into our lives.

". . . where the Spirit of the Lord is, there is freedom" (2 Cor. 3:17, RSV).

[1] John R. Claypool, "Sin, Identity, and Power" (A sermon given at North-minster Baptist Church, Jackson, Mississippi, Feb. 6, 1977).
[2] Bernard Ramm, *Them He Glorified* (Grand Rapids: Wm. B. Eerdmans Publishing Company, 1963), pp. 80-83.

To Think About:

1. What kinds of failure are evident in your own life? Perhaps the following common ones will stimulate your thinking!

—Lack of concern for other people.

—Negative attitudes about yourself, about life, about other people, about God.

—Failure to develop your talents, your personal assets.

—Failure to be a responsible father or mother.

—Failure to be the right husband or wife.

—Failure to take care of your body—exercise, eating habits, rest, recreation.

Do these failures constitute sin?

2. Are you aware of the pull to go the wrong way in your life? Is it subtle or powerful? Can you handle it by yourself, or do you need God's help?

3. Is there an exciting sense of freedom in your life? Are you one of those Christians who feels really free to become all that God created you to be?

4. If you don't have a sense of Christian freedom, can you pinpoint the cause? What can you do about it?

9
The Child of God Gets Tender Loving Care

Romans 8

Most of us grew up in rather normal, healthy families. We knew how we were expected to act as children in the family. There were certain things we were supposed to do; there were other things we definitely were not allowed to do. We also knew what to expect from our parents.

In chapter 8 of Romans, Paul talks about what we can expect as children in the family of God. He says we can count on the ultimate in tender loving care if we are true children of God.

But Paul puts a condition on qualifying as a child of God. First we are warned that "Any one who does not have the Spirit of Christ does not belong to him" (Rom. 8:9, RSV). Then we are told, "For all who are led by the Spirit of God are sons of God" (v. 14, RSV). Are we willing to be led along by God's Spirit? Once we have met that condition, we are assured of our place in God's household.

"You have been adopted into the very family circle of God and you can say with a full heart, 'Father, my Father.' The Spirit himself endorses our inward conviction that we really are the children of God. Think what that means. If we are his children then we are God's heirs, and all that Christ inherits will belong to all of us as well!" (vv. 15-17, Phillips).

It's exciting to think about the treasures Paul says
we share in God's family. He does not explain what
they are, but he does spell out for us some of the things
that are in store for us as God's children. Let me recount
them for you in terms of "heaves and sighs!"

When I was studying music history in college, Wagner's music was lightly described as "heaves and sighs."
This is not a bad description of life in general when
we consider that "heave" means to do something with
great effort and we commonly speak of "sighs of relief"
and "sighs of contentment." "Heave" can also mean
an upward motion—and a sigh can signal a time of
rest.

Paul's description of the Christian life falls into the
category of "heaves and sighs." There are times of
great effort and there are times of rest and reassurance.
Some people might think this also fits well into the out-
line of popular stories about "good news and bad news."

I prefer to describe it in terms of "heaves and sighs."
Ready? Look at verses 3-16 in Romans 8.

Heave: There is an ongoing battle to fight. How good
are you at fighting battles? Most of us have had experience of one kind or another—and much of it we gained
within the family circle! We grew up fighting with brothers and sisters.

In God's family, though, the battle should not be with
one another. The Bible points out where the real struggle is: It's within ourselves. It's the struggle with sin
which Paul described in Romans 7.

In Romans 8 Paul describes the battle as a struggle
between the "flesh" and the "spirit." By "flesh" (the
Greek word is *sarx*), he means not only the human body,

but selfish human desires—the shortsighted wants of the human psyche. If we are controlled by them, we may think we are pleasing ourselves, but Paul says that these selfish desires are the same ones that once were leading us to death (v. 6). And that is not what we want at all.

Although we belong to God, sin continues to exert a powerful pull in our lives; our human wants continue to cry out. Does this mean that our natural cravings are wrong? Must we deny our basic human desires?

Let me share with you a friend's definition of sin: "Sin . . . is man denying his deepest capacity and calling, spurning God's offer of employment, going into business for himself with the capital that God has given him, and at last becoming a destructive competitor with God." [1]

Our human desires are part of the capital that God has given us. They become sinful only when they come into destructive competition with God. We all desire love, achievement, recognition, and security. All our basic needs cry out to be met. God wants them to be met within his good plan for us. We are tempted to satisfy them in unhealthy and destructive ways.

Since God has set us free from sin and death (Rom. 8:2), we do not *have* to sin. But the *temptation* to sin is still there—so the struggle goes on.

Sigh: God's Spirit gives us the power and the guidance we need to be winners. Once we were powerless (weak, helpless) (Rom. 5:6). But God's Spirit is the most powerful force in the world. The Hebrew word for spirit is *ruach:* this is also the word for "wind." Wind is powerful. On the day of Pentecost the Holy Spirit came with a sound like "the rush of a mighty wind" (Acts

2:2, RSV). The Spirit's power raised Jesus from the dead (Rom. 8:11). That power is available to us.

God's Spirit is also gentle. Jesus called him the "Comforter" or "Counselor." He said, "I will pray the Father, and he will give you another Counselor, to be with you for ever, even the Spirit of truth" (John 14:16-17, RSV). He helps us to know the truth about God, about ourselves, about the world, about God's plan for us in the world (see John 14-16). This frees us from the deception of sin which we talked about in the last chapter. With God's Spirit to be our counselor and to give us power, we can win the battle with sin.

What else can we expect as children of God?

Heave: We may not win every battle, but—

Sigh: We will never be condemned for our failures. This is another "good news" aspect of the ongoing battle. We will never be condemned, even though we may lose the battle from time to time. Paul begins chapter 8 by saying, "There is therefore now no condemnation to them which are in Christ Jesus, who walk not after the flesh, but after the Spirit" (Rom. 8:1, KJV). Later he substantiates the same idea: "Who would dare to accuse us, whom God has chosen? God himself has declared us free from sin. Who is in a position to condemn? Only Christ Jesus, and Christ died for us, Christ also rose for us, . . . Christ prays for us!" (Rom. 8:33-34, Phillips).

God does not condemn us. Other people have no right to condemn us (they are losing some battles too). We shouldn't live in fear that we may not measure up as children of God; instead we should live our lives freely, without fear, precisely because we are beloved children of God himself. "For you did not receive the spirit of slavery to fall back into fear, but you have received the spirit of sonship" (Rom. 8:15, RSV).

What should we do when we lose the battle? We are disappointed in ourselves; we feel guilty about failing to measure up. Our own conscience, our own spirit, condemns us. What can we do?

When we have failed, it's important to deal with the guilt feeling as soon as possible. We have departed from God's way. We must express our sorrow to God for having strayed from his guidance. Ask him to bring you back to his way. Talk to him freely about your failure; spend time listening to his words (the Bible) to you. Experience his love, his forgiveness, his understanding. Experience the power of his Spirit in your life. You will feel strong and whole again.

Of course, you did not have to lose the battle (see 1 Cor. 10:13). Let the experience help you to be better prepared next time.

And remember, "There is . . . no condemnation"—(sigh!).

Heave: We must share the suffering of Christ. That is another condition. Verse 17 says we are heirs with Christ "provided we suffer with him in order that we may also be glorified with him" (RSV). Some commentators say this does not mean the ordinary suffering everyone experiences in the world (affliction, illness and so on), but only suffering that is unique to the Christian—suffering that comes as a result of persecution because we are Christians.

It seems to me that suffering with Christ means loving people as he did and being rejected by them as he was. It also means identifying with those who suffer, taking up their cause, sharing in their suffering. It means being in close union with Christ so that we too feel responsible to do something about the hurt in the world.

Can we seek suffering? We cannot seek to be a martyr, but we can seek to love people—knowing full well that the more we love, the more likely we are to suffer rejection and misunderstanding.

Any suffering we bear patiently in the strength of God, with the help of the Spirit, brings us into special fellowship with Christ. He was well-acquainted with suffering and grief. Hebrews 5:8 says, "Although he was a Son, he learned obedience through what he suffered" (RSV). If this was true of Jesus, surely it is true of us. We are also told that suffering teaches us endurance and develops Christian character (see chap. 6 for Scripture references). The Christian life is tough. Any kind of trouble can be a time of hard testing for the Christian. One of the results, of course, is God's glory, which we discussed also in chapter 6. And Paul says, "In my opinion whatever we may have to go through now is less than nothing compared with the magnificent future God has planned for us" (Rom. 8:18, Phillips).

So much for the bad news! What other good things can we expect when we are led by the Spirit?

Sigh: The Holy Spirit helps us with all our weaknesses (see Rom. 8:26). Every life has weaknesses. They may be in the areas of pride, honesty, sex, greed, temper, hostility, or any number of other personality or character traits. Some "weaknesses" may be physical—illness, for example; others may be emotional—perhaps depression or distrust of others. The word that is translated "weaknesses" in the Revised Standard Version is translated "infirmities" in the King James Version and "limitations" in Phillips' New Testament.

Sometimes we need help with our strengths as well as our weaknesses. If we feel we are really good in an area or that we are proficient at doing a particular thing, the tendency may be to reject God's help in that area; we can handle it ourselves.

Whatever our problem is, the same mighty power that raised Jesus from the grave is available to help us—either to overcome the weakness entirely or to handle it in a way that brings glory to the Father.

Sigh: The Holy Spirit helps us with our praying (see Rom. 8:26-27). Jesus promised that if we ask him or the Father to meet our needs, they will be met (see, for example, John 14:13-14; John 16:23-24). Throughout the New Testament we are urged to pray fervently and confidently (see Jas. 5:16-18 and Heb. 4:16, for examples). Paul says the Holy Spirit teaches us how to pray, but he does more than that. When our needs are so overwhelming that we are at a loss even to voice them, the Holy Spirit actually does our praying with us and for us. He knows what God is already longing to give us, and he pleads in our stead for God to give us just that! How is that for tender loving care?

The kindness of God is almost unbelievable! Paul gives us another promise about what we can expect as children of God.

Sigh: God can bring good out of every situation. This is not a magic act. He wants us always to experience the best in our lives; but the actual promise, is that God will work *with us* to bring about the benefits. "We know that in everything God works for good with those who love him, who are called according to his

purpose" (Rom. 8:28, RSV). Phillips translates the verse
this way: "Moreover we know that to those who love
God, who are called according to his plan, everything
that happens fits into a pattern for good."

Another *sigh* of contentment: *God will give us every-*
thing we need. He may not give us all our wants, because that might not be good for us, but he will give
us all that we really need. Here is what Paul says:
"In face of all this, what is there left to say? If God
is for us, who can be against us? He who did not grudge
his own Son but gave him up for us all—can we not
trust such a God to give us, with him, everything else
that we can need?" (8:31-32, Phillips).

There is one final thing we can always depend on
as children of God. *Sigh of ecstasy! Nothing can ever*
separate us from his complete, overwhelming, uncon-
ditional love. We talked about that in chapter 7. Paul
expresses it again here in beautiful, poetic language
as he describes the love of God in Christ.

> Who can separate us from the love of Christ?
> Can trouble, pain or persecution? Can lack of
> clothes and food, danger to life and limb, the threat
> of force of arms? . . . .
>
> No, in all these things we win an over-whelming
> victory through him who has proved his love for
> us.
>
> I have become absolutely convinced that neither
> death nor life, neither messenger of Heaven nor
> monarch of earth, neither what happens today nor
> what may happen tomorrow, neither a power from
> on high nor a power from below, nor anything else
> in God's whole world has any power to separate

us from the love of God in Christ Jesus our Lord! (Rom. 8:35-39, Phillips).

[1] J. Lyn Elder, "Christianity as a Way of Love: An Experiment in Pastoral Theology" (unpublished manuscript used by Dr. Elder in his classes at Golden Gate Baptist Seminary).

To Think About:

1. In your own life, how do you "follow after" the Holy Spirit? Is it a satisfying experience for you?

2. Are you tolerant of the way other people interpret how to live in the Spirit, or do you get defensive when others explain what their own "Spirit-filled life" is like?

3. In what way have you personally experienced the "treasures" of God?

4. How is your prayer life? Do you allow the Holy Spirit to help you with your praying?

To Do:

If guilt has been a problem for you, read:

Paul Tournier, *Guilt and Grace.* New York: Harper & Row Publishers 1962.

10
Would God Choose You?

Romans 9 and 10

When children choose sides for games at school, it becomes apparent right away which children are capable or well-liked and which are not. The child who is chosen first or second feels reassured, but the child who is consistently left until last suffers hurt and rejection. Can you recall how important it was to be chosen?

In Romans 9—11 Paul talks about the people God has chosen. These three chapters (the middle section of Romans) comprise Paul's thoughts and feelings about the Jewish race—his own people. He shares his anguish about their rejection of Jesus and their failure to carry out their responsibilities.

A Jew was very proud of being a Jew—one of God's choice ones. You are probably aware that the Jews glumped all the other people in the world together as Gentiles. To a Jew there were, in a sense, only two classes of people—Jews (the fortunate people of the world) and non-Jews (the unfortunate people). The Jews sometimes referred to non-Jews rather contemptuously (or piteously) as "Gentile dogs."

The Jewish race began when God made his promise to Abraham: "And I will make of thee a great nation, and I will bless thee, and make thy name great; . . .

and in thee shall all families of the earth be blessed"
(Gen. 12:2-3, KJV).

Abraham and Sarah's only child was Isaac, and he
inherited the agreement with God.

Isaac, in turn, had two sons, Esau and Jacob. They
were twins, but Esau was considered the elder, because
he was born first. He should, according to the custom
of the day, have received the family inheritance and
the blessing. Instead, you remember, Jacob managed
to get both of them—mainly because they were really
important to him.

God had already told their mother before the twins
were born what the score would be. He said, "The elder
shall serve the younger" (Gen. 25:23, KJV).

This is Paul's account of what happened: "And then,
again, a word of promise came to Rebecca, at the time
when she was pregnant with two children. . . . It came
before the children were born or had done anything
good or bad, plainly showing that God's act of choice
has nothing to do with achievements, but is entirely a
matter of his will."

She was told: "The elder shall serve the younger"
(Rom. 9:10-12, Phillips).

God's choice of Jacob might be explained, at least
partially, by divine foresight. Was Jacob chosen because
God could foresee that Jacob would be responsive to
him when Esau would not be? Was it because he knew
in advance that Jacob would call on him? At any rate,
God dealt in a special way with Jacob.

Jacob didn't really deserve God's blessings, because
in his younger days Jacob got what he could by "hook
or crook." He cheated and lied. But when he was really
up against it, he placed himself in God's hands, and

God changed him. So the divine promise passed to Jacob
and all his descendants; they became the Israelites or
Jews.

You've probably heard the couplet:

How odd of God
To choose the Jews.

Have you felt that way about some of the people God
has chosen to bless or to use? God frequently chooses
people whom we would reject. We can see that some
of them don't deserve to be chosen! Their lives leave
much to be desired or their personalities are bother-
some. Sometimes even their theology is off-base. Why
doesn't God stick with people who are acceptable?

Two points are obvious from reading these chapters.
The first is the same fact which Jacob illustrated: God
can choose anyone he pleases, bless and use that person,
regardless of whether he deserves it. Of course, if you'll
check the biblical records, you'll see that God usually
chooses those who will believe and follow him. He does
not necessarily choose the good people. Good people
may not be responsive at all to God; they are sometimes
self-satisfied. They may not want to follow God's leading or allow him to remold them for his purposes.

Another concept in this chapter is that we can't win
God's favor by living an impressive life. That's one mis-
take some of the Jewish leaders were into during the
time of Christ. They went around trying to impress
God and everyone else by showing how well they kept
the religious rules and regulations.

But God was not impressed. He was not looking for
religious people. He was looking for people who knew
they needed his help—people who would open their
hearts to him. These were the people who responded

to Jesus and who received him into their lives as the very Son of God.

Paul's message in these chapters is that God does the choosing—and he chooses those who put their faith in Christ.

> If you declare with your lips, "Jesus is Lord," and believe in your heart that God raised him from the dead, you will be saved . . . . The scripture says, "Whoever believes in him will not be disappointed." This includes everyone, for there is no difference between Jews and Gentiles; God is the same Lord of all and richly blesses everyone who calls on him (Rom. 10:9-12, TEV).

Notice especially the last part of verse 12: "God . . . richly blesses everyone who calls on him." Jacob called on him. So can you.

What are we chosen for? God chooses us, first of all for salvation—a continual process of being remade. Then he calls us to do his work. "You did not choose me, but I chose you and appointed you that you should go and bear fruit and that your fruit should abide" (John 15:16, RSV).

God does not usually hand us some great earthshaking task as our first assignment (although he could). Ordinarily we begin in small ways. "Whoever is faithful in small matters will be faithful in large ones; whoever is dishonest in small matters will be dishonest in large ones. If, then, you have not been faithful in handling worldly wealth, how can you be trusted with true wealth?" (Luke 16:10-11, TEV).

If you want to do great things in this life, be faithful

with the responsibilities you now have. Are you a responsible student, career person, homemaker? Are you conscientious in letting Christ share these responsibilities? How faithfully do you "seek his kingdom" in the everyday happenings of your life? If you are faithful in the small matters, they can be great beginnings in God's kingdom.

There are certain responsibilities which go along with whatever God has chosen you for. Let's consider some of them:

1. Honor the relationship. When God chooses us for a specific task, the job is never more important than the relationship with him. In fact, we cannot carry out the assignment apart from that relationship. Jesus said, "I am the vine you are the branches. He who abides in me, and I in him, he it is that bears much fruit for apart from me you can do nothing. If a man does not abide in me, he is cast forth as a branch and withers; and the branches are gathered, thrown into the fire and burned" (John 15:5-6, RSV).

Your intimate friendship with Christ is the most important obligation of your life.

2. Follow his instructions. The followers of Christ are always in apprenticeship on this earth. We are always in need of learning, of developing, of being open and responsive. We are responsible for carrying out the instructions of Christ who said, "love one another," and "keep my commandments."

He also said, "When you obey me, you are living in my love, just as I obey my Father and live in his love. I have told you this so that you will be filled with my joy. Yes, your cup of joy will overflow!" (John 15:10-11, TLB).

3. Be faithful. Some people love the honor of being chosen for a job but hate doing the work involved. What can I say about that? Only that when you agree to take an assignment, you have agreed to do the work. When it is truly God's assignment, he has already given us or will give us the ability to do the job. We have but to obey him.

But there is that tendency in most of us to slough off. It is often easier to let the real work go while we busy ourselves with other more or less useful tasks that are thrown our way. Or it's easy to be distracted by other enjoyable pastimes. Jesus' parable toward the end of Matthew 24 about the unfaithful servant is a good reminder to us that we are to watch for our Master's return. Whether it is his final return to earth or simply his personal return to the individual, we have been warned to be ready. That means we are to be faithfully doing our assignment.

4. Be concerned about others. Did you notice Paul's intense concern for the Jewish people in Romans 9:1-3? Phillips translated it this way: "Before Christ and my own conscience in the Holy Spirit I assure you that I am speaking the plain truth when I say that there is something that makes me feel very depressed, like a pain that never leaves me. It is the condition of my brothers and fellow-Israelites, and I have actually reached the pitch of wishing myself cut off from Christ if it meant that they could be won for God."

The Jerusalem Bible renders verses 2-3 like this: ". . . My sorrow is so great, my mental anguish so endless, I would willingly be condemned and be cut off from Christ if it could help my brothers of Israel, my own flesh and blood." [1]

This mental anguish is certainly outweighed by the joy that Paul expresses throughout his writings. But it reminds us of our own responsibility toward non-Christians. Paul says again in Romans 10:1: "My brothers, how I wish with all my heart that my own people might be saved! How I pray to God for them!" (TEV). Of course not everyone who hears the good news accepts it, but Paul reminds us in Romans 10:16-21 that God keeps on reaching out his hands to people, even when they are unresponsive. And so should we.

[1] *The Jerusalem Bible,* (Garden City, New York: Doubleday and Company, Inc., 1966).

For Thought:

1. Compare Paul's concern for the Jews with your own concern for family members or friends who have a deep need for God's help in their lives.

2. Are you aware that God has chosen you and blessed you in unexpected ways? What has he chosen you to do?

3. Does it bother you when God chooses someone else and blesses that person in ways he obviously doesn't deserve? Is this a matter of envy?

4. What do you do to keep your relationship to Christ up-to-date?

5. Do you ever try to earn God's favor? How?

11
Practice the Wide-Eyed Look

Romans 11

If you read the newspapers, you are aware of the many hopeless situations in our world today. Some of these concern nations, others concern individuals. When we look at our world in general—nations lined up against nations—we can understand the feeling of despair that descends on many people.

Some of you face situations in your own lives that appear hopeless. What can you do when you've done your best, and it looks as if there's no improvement? Sometimes we begin to feel that we should give up the battle.

That's the way Elijah felt when he had given his best years to delivering God's message to the Israelites. He spoke out bravely against a wicked king and queen, but God's people didn't listen. More and more of them began forsaking God and worshiping Baal. Elijah was beginning to feel that he was the only one left who was true to God.

Paul could have had the same feeling of despair about the Jews' refusal to accept Jesus. For generations they had expected the Messiah, and when he came they wouldn't have him. But Paul learned a lesson from Elijah.

Paul didn't play the game of I'm-the-only-one. Do you

ever play that game? It's played from time to time at
our house. Why am I the only one who sets the table?
Why am I the only one who has to practice music?
I'm the only one who didn't get to go!

On the grown-up level, it's more often played within
ourselves: Why am I the one who always loses? I'm
the only one who never gets consulted.

In Romans 11 Paul continues his discourse about the
Jewish people. Here's the story he relates about God's
prophet who thought he was the only one.

Elijah had just had that mountain-top experience
where he exercised his faith—put everything on the
line—by challenging the prophets of Baal to a contest
between Baal and God. If you are not familiar with
the story, read it in 1 Kings 18—19.

Elijah won a great victory that day. God proved that
he was the only God, and all the prophets of Baal were
wiped out. But as a result, the wicked Queen Jezebel
vowed to have Elijah's life within a day's time.

Elijah was afraid and went into a deep depression.
He asked God to take his life. At God's direction he
went off by himself to Mount Horeb and moved into
a cave. Then God began to communicate with him. First
there was a windstorm, then an earthquake, then a fire.

Finally Elijah heard the calm, quiet voice of God. He
emerged from the cave and stated his complaint to God:
"The people of Israel have forsaken thy covenant,
thrown down thy altars, and slain thy prophets with
the sword; and I, even I only, am left; and they seek
my life, to take it away" (1 Kings 19:14, RSV).

God answered by giving Elijah some instructions.
"Here's what I have for you to do now," he said in
essence. Then tacked on to the end of the instructions:

"And incidentally, there are 7,000 men in Israel who
have never bowed to Baal" (v. 18, TLB).

No doubt, 7,000 was a minority—even a small minority. But they were a few more people than just Elijah.
Those 7,000 were probably at home praising God for
the victory they'd seen on Mount Carmel. Why do you
suppose Elijah was unaware of them? Was he so
wrapped up in his own mission that he was totally oblivi-
ous to the *other* people whose hearts were right with
the Lord? He wasn't the only one.

Paul's point in relating the story of Elijah was to
say he (Paul) wasn't the only Jew who had accepted
the Messiah. There were other people who were just
as Jewish and just as Christian as Paul was. He was
keeping his eyes open to reality even in the face of a
depressing situation. He pointed to hope when things
might have appeared hopeless. Perhaps we can learn
something from Paul and Elijah.

*Keep your eyes open to see God working in the
lives of others.* God always has some people who remain
true to him—whether we're speaking of nations, races,
denominations, or churches. People are there who belong to him, and God is at work in their lives. Look
out for these people. Listen to their testimony. They
will lift your spirit.

Keep your eyes open to the bigness of God's plan.
The Jews appeared to have "blown it" because they
rejected Jesus, but Paul says God is still in charge.
He is bringing order out of the situation. He will work
another way to carry out his purpose. His plan was
bigger than the Jewish race. It was bigger than the
Roman Empire. It's always bigger than we imagine it
to be. New developments are up ahead.

Keep your eyes open to your own position. Paul concludes his long discourse in chapters 9—11 by reminding the Roman Christians (Gentiles) to keep their humility. Using the metaphor of an olive tree, he says in essence, "Don't look down your branches at the Jews because of their failure. You are included in God's plan only by your faith, so hang on to your humility."

Humility is not a popular word in our assertive world today, but it is an important word to remember in our relationship to God. Here are some words from him:

"My thoughts," says the Lord, "are not like yours, and my ways are different from yours. As high as the heavens are above the earth, so high are my ways and thoughts above yours" (Isa. 55:8-9, TEV).

"Now remember what you were, brothers, when God called you. Few of you were wise, or powerful, or of high social standing, from the human point of view" (1 Cor. 1:26, TEV).

It's possible for us to exhibit some of the same attitudes that caused God's chosen people to fail.

1. *"I'm superior!"* Sometimes this is exhibited as racial prejudice; at other times it is personal "delusions of grandeur." When we are chosen by God, we may forget that we were meant to bring happiness to the people around us. The Jews began to refer to non-Jews as "Gentile dogs." God's direction to be "set apart," to be different from their neighbors, became misdirected into an attitude of exclusiveness: "We're better than others." God had said, "I will bless you so that you will be a blessing."

Feelings of superiority should not be replaced by false humility. Let me illustrate. False humility would say, "I'm inferior." This is not true. Jesus proved we were worth a great, great price. We are contradicting all that he came for if we believe that we are inferior. Instead, we should recognize our worth and respect God for all that he has done for us by trying to live as he wants us to—by helping those around us.

2. *"I've arrived!"* The Jewish people seemed to feel (at least during some periods of their history) that since God had chosen them, they couldn't possibly do anything wrong. God would provide for them, protect them, and never turn them away. They had it made! Following God's directions became unimportant while they "did their own thing." As a result, they wandered far away from God's purpose for them. They were thinking, "My place is guaranteed, and I don't have to worry about it."

False humility might say, "My place is unimportant." Wrong, of course. Your place is strategic. Keep closely in touch with God. Follow his instructions so that you won't do something disappointing just when he's counting on you.

3. *"I'll do it my way!"* At another period in Jewish history, the people tried to impress God—especially one another—by seeing who could keep each detail of the Jewish rules and regulations. "Who can be the most religious?" became their game of life. They were playing it their way instead of God's way.

Sometimes we try to impress everyone, including God, by the way we do our work (or his work). Our goal may be to be more creative, more sophisticated, more dedicated, more intellectual, more helpful. We have our own ideas about the way things ought to be done—about what is or is not an effective ministry, about what should or should not be done to help someone else. Consult other capable people. God may have another blueprint.

That does not mean your way is no good, or that your ideas are not the best. God gave you your abilities; he can help you make the most of them.

Elijah mistakenly thought he was the only one being true to God. He felt like the only one in such an unfortunate situation. He was wrong, of course. Neither are you the only one in your particular circumstance. But you are the only one of your kind. You are the only one who can carry out God's plan for you. And it's a good plan. You are the only one who can fill your place, and it's an important place. You are the only one who has your unique talents and abilities; use them with God's guidance. Rejoice that God has chosen you!

To Think About:

1. Have you observed God at work lately in your own life or someone else's?

2. Another word for "humble" might be "teachable." How much does this attitude enter into your relationship with God?

3. Are there discouraging times in your life when you can't discern God's plan? What do you do during these times?

12
What Kind of Body Are You?

Romans 12:1

I confess that I don't know a lot about bodies, although I've been one for many years. I know that bodies are sometimes nuisances because they break down, get out of shape, and do annoying things. We spend hundreds of dollars trying to keep them feeling and acting as we want them to.

I also know that psychologists are concerned about the number of people who "betray" their bodies. They ignore or deny how they feel and how they look, while they stubbornly carry on a lifestyle that isn't right for them. Only a serious illness (physical or emotional) can get their attention.

There are people, of course, who take their bodies very seriously. They lift weights, do exercises, run miles, and eat carefully so that everything will stay in good shape. They are concerned about being healthy, feeling well, and looking good. Good for them!

Others are concerned only about how their body looks. Exercising and eating sensibly may be part of their regimen, but only for visible improvement. The main concern is appearance. That means beauty treatments, hair styling, face lifts, capped teeth, and fashionable clothes.

Some people become slaves to their bodies. They bow

down to every ache and pain. Each day's activities may be changed or modified to take their "feelings" into account.

All this preoccupation with the body often turns out to be superficial. The body is an intricate union of physical, mental, and spiritual forces. We have to go inside the body—into the mind and spirit—and attend to things there also if we want to be whole.

Bodies are important in the Christian belief. Many religions aim to overcome the body or to become free from it. Only Christianity, Judaism, and Islam attach any ultimate value to the body.[1] These religions look forward to a resurrection. The great point of the resurrection itself is that we will be bodies again—as if we cannot be complete without them, as if we cannot fully experience all the joys of heaven without bodies.

Of course, Christianity is the only religion in which God himself became a body. It was a body that was crucified; it was a body that rose again; it was a body that ascended into heaven (although a transformed one). And all of us are familiar with the sacred words, "This is my body." The Christian church itself is called a "body" of believers. We represent the body of Christ in the world.

When God made our bodies they were good and of value. They still are. It's too bad they are so often misunderstood, commercialized and exploited, ignored and mistreated, and burdened with guilt and discouragement.

In Romans 12 Paul deals with the practical aspects of the Christian life—how does one *live* as a Christian? He deals with growing healthy Christian personalities. And he begins by pleading with the Roman Christians to give their bodies to God. They were already Christians, of course. Yet Paul says, "I urge you, I beg you, I plead with you [compare the various translations] to give your bodies to God."

A strange request, is it not? Had these Christians spiritualized their relationship with Christ so that it had little practical application? Had they given their "souls"—some nebulous, holy part of themselves—to God, thinking that was all he required?

When Paul said, "Give your body to God," he meant give the real you, the you that you live and work with day after day. You are physical, mental, and spiritual, but all that you experience, you experience in your body.

"I appeal to you therefore, . . . by the mercies of God to present your bodies as a living sacrifice" (Rom. 12:1, RSV).

When the Hebrew people brought a sacrifice to God, it was the best they had to offer—an animal they were proud of that was killed and laid on the altar. It was a symbol of the person's serious desire to please God—to live as God wanted him to live.

Paul is asking us to offer God our very best selves, our bodies. But this is to be a *living* sacrifice, not a dead one.

What are you giving when you give yourself to God? You are giving your physical appearance, your emotions, your intelligence, your talents, your energy to God. You are giving God all that you are—both in your inner being and in your outward expression.

When I was entering adolescence, my body became my number one problem. I was already feeling slightly awkward and unattractive; I was becoming a Twiggy in the days of Marilyn Monroe. Then my family moved, and I entered a new school away from the support of my old friends. Right away I was labeled a "brain," which I would not have been in the more competitive school I came from. This caused problems, of course. But the worst problem was one I couldn't figure out. My body began to tremble. At any time of stress or self-consciousness, I trembled visibly. I overcame this somewhat as I grew older and began to regain some of my confidence. But what a relief it was many years later when I was treated for hyperthyroid. No more worry about trembling. For years, all my social relationships had been colored by that embarrassment.

No doubt my problem was as much psychological as physical. My body was reflecting my deep fear of rejection. No amount of praying brought about a miracle. I had given myself to God for better or worse, and for a teenager, this was definitely worse.

And yet I was constantly aware that this was not God's will for me. He did not want me to be bound by fear and apprehension. My hope and stability was the firm assurance that good things were ahead for me; God had a plan for my life. I must prepare to be what he wanted me to be. That assurance saw me through some discouraging years.

During that time, God seldom waved his magic wand and gave me a steady body, but he taught me many things about depending on him, about compassion, about the "renewing of the mind." I spent more time than I otherwise might have in reflection and meditation. I was getting better acquainted not only with God but also with myself.

I would probably have denied my insecurities if my body had not attested to them so visibly. This is one of the current messages of psychology: Pay attention to your body; it will tell you a lot about yourself.

Some psychologists say, "Get in touch with your feelings." This is another way of saying, "Get in touch with your body," because that is where we experience our feelings. Emotions are felt in the throat, in the heart, in the reproductive organs, in the pit of the stomach.

If we do not acknowledge our emotions, we become alienated from them. If I refuse to admit to myself that I'm angry, my anger will show up as a headache or a stomachache, or as some behavior that I don't understand. It will surely be felt in muscular tension. How much better it is if I recognize it and deal with it constructively.

How many people do you know who work very hard during the day and then at night tune out all personal thoughts and feelings by watching television? No wonder they don't know who they really are.

Sometimes we deny feelings because we're trying to live up to an image. Too many Christians, I'm afraid, carry a mental image of what the Christian should be, and they try to fit themselves into that image. They ignore their own emotions and needs in a futile attempt to "be what they ought to be."

That is not to say that an image has no value. We have all benefited from good examples of the Christian life. But we can't be like some Christian we have known. Our feelings tell us who we are and what is real for us. The Holy Spirit guides us to develop in our own way.

The authentic feelings of the Christian should not be fear, guilt, hate, and inferiority. All of these are negatives. But all of us have known these feelings to some extent, and we can't be true to ourselves by denying them. When we give ourselves to God, we give him our negative feelings. He will help us to deal with them. Sometimes this includes seeking the help of a qualified counselor.

Negative emotions may be deep-rooted and require a period of time to overcome; learning to express them properly is part of the healing process. Healing the sick and freeing the captives are very real aspects of the Christian ministry. Too many of us neglect the responsibility of seeking healing and freedom for our bodies when they are bound by negative emotions.

What are the dominant emotions of the Christian life? They are love, joy, and peace. These arise out of a sense of well-being. They come as a result of being loved and of feeling our sense of worth to God and to others. These are the emotions we want to plug into. Love, happiness, satisfaction, peace, pleasure, joy, exuberance—positive emotions. If we are missing these, we are not really living. Jesus said, "I came that they may have life, and have it abundantly" (John 10:10, RSV).

What are you feeling these days? Can you verbalize your feelings to someone? Can you express them on paper? Can you express them to God? Get in touch with your feelings, because you are what you feel.

You are, of course, much more than you feel. You are your memories and all your past experiences. You are how you look; you are what you habitually do. You are all the personal attributes and abilities that God has given you.

I hope that when you think about giving these to God, you do not think only in terms of church or of religious situations. Most of the time your body is in the world. It's in your home. It's on the job. It's in a meeting. It's playing tennis. It's running or going for a hike. It's making love; it's eating a meal, driving a car, going to bed. "Whatever you do, do all to the glory of God" (1 Cor. 10:31, RSV).

Love, joy, and peace free your body from tensions and hang-ups. They are gifts of God's Spirit, who can make you more alive than you've ever been before. "I appeal to you therefore, brethren, by the mercies of God, to present your bodies as a living sacrifice, holy and acceptable to God, which is your spiritual worship" (Rom. 12:1, RSV).

Our motivation for giving ourselves to God is his "mercies"—all that he has done for us and will continue to do for us. The sacrifice that we give him will be "holy."

The Greek word for "holy" simply meant to be set apart for a particular purpose, or set apart for God. In Christian writings it also carries the idea of being righteous or free from sin. We can be free from sin only by God's mercy—because of what he has done for us in Christ. The Christian can be described as holy to the extent that God dwells within him. "Do you not know that you are God's temple and that God's Spirit dwells in you?" (1 Cor. 3:16, RSV). This is our guarantee of being acceptable to God.

It is hard to explain what is meant by "spiritual worship." C. K. Barrett suggests that in Judaism there was a service of the altar and there was also a service of the heart. After the destruction of the Temple in A.D. 70 it was said that, though other sacrifices had ceased, the sacrifice of praise and thanksgiving remained.[2] Paul may have had this in mind when he wrote of the Christian's spiritual worship.

Barrett also notes that, in a famous passage, Epictetus declared, "If I were a nightingale I would do what is proper to a nightingale . . .; but in fact I am a rational creature, so I must praise God."

Our bodies, our personalities, our way of life should be a praise song to God. It should be offered as naturally as the nightingale offers his song. Giving ourselves as a sacrifice to God means that we no longer live for our own short-sighted glory, but for the greater glory of God.

[1] See John Y. Fenton, "Bodily Theology," and Bernard Aaronson, "The Experience of the Body and Transcendence," in *Theology and Body*, ed. John Y. Fenton (Philadelphia: The Westminster Press, 1974), pp. 46,130-35.

[2] C. K. Barrett, *The Epistle to the Romans*, Harper's New Testament Commentaries (New York: Harper & Brothers, Publishers, 1958), p. 232.

To Think About and Do:

1. Your appearance is the first way you communicate with others. Your "looks" tell them who you are. Are you really familiar with how you look—your posture, your facial expression, your style of dress? Does your appearance communicate what you want to say?

2. Do you know how your voice sounds? Does it tell you anything about yourself?

3. Describe yourself in a paragraph or two. Make it completely positive. Mention your good features. Don't say anything derogatory about yourself.

4. List four or five emotions that you are aware of

experiencing in the past week. Are they positive or negative emotions?

5. Which areas of your life have you given to God? Which ones are you holding back?

To Read:

William R. Parker and Elaine St. Johns, *Prayer Can Change Your Life.* New York: Cornerstone Library, 1974.

13
Don't Be a Cheap Copy When You Can Be an Original Design

Romans 12:2

Recently in Marin County, California, a young art dealer was caught defrauding people of thousands of dollars by selling them *copies* of valuable art. Unsuspecting people sunk large chunks of their savings into what they thought would be a solid investment. How disillusioning and embarrassing to find out they had invested in copies instead of originals.

What about your life? Is it a disappointing copy of someone else's idea? Paul has something to say about the original you. "Don't copy the behavior and customs of this world, but be a new and different person with a fresh newness in all you do and think" (Rom. 12:2*a*, TLB).

Paul begins Romans 12 by asking us to give our bodies to God. He follows this by confronting us with our Christian identity. He does not draw up a stereotype and say, "All Christians should be like this." Once we have presented ourselves to God, we have begun a process of identification. We have been set on the road of finding out who we really are and how we can best fulfill our own role in life (not the role that somebody else gives us).

Paul expresses ideas such as: "don't give in to the pressures and customs around you" (v. 2); "be honest

90

in forming an opinion of yourself" (v. 3); "your gifts are uniquely your own; use them enthusiastically" (vv. 6-8, author's translation).

He goes on to say something like: "love is important; work is important; people are important; approach life positively" (vv. 9-21, author's translation). Paul is picturing Christians who are developing strong and healthy Christian personalities. He is describing persons who are sure of themselves and their place in the world.

Our society is characterized by what some psychologists call "identity confusion." People are not certain who they are. We have lost touch with how we feel, and we're confused about what we want to be. We tend to imitate other people and try to do what is expected of us.

An "identity crisis" is to be expected in adolescence and young adulthood. But it is something we hope to overcome as we find our place in the world.

In *Dimensions of a New Identity*, Erik H. Erikson says, "In youth you find out what you *care to do* and who you *care to be.* . . ."[1] But many people fail to find out those very things.

According to psychiatrist Alexander Lowen, some of us are confused about our identity because of the way we were brought up. Too many families today live with the idea of fulfilling an image. The children are taught to live up to the image of success, of popularity, of sex appeal, of intellectual snobbery, of status—even of self-sacrifice. Alexander Lowen says sooner or later an identity based on images and roles fails to provide satisfaction. The image is "an abstraction, an ideal, and an idol which demands the sacrifice of personal feeling."

A person attempting to fulfill even an image he has chosen for himself "feels frustrated and cheated of emotional satisfaction." [2] We were not created to be always play-acting!

Kenneth S. Wuest's translation of Romans 12:2 seems to speak particularly well to this current problem. It urges us to find our true identity. "Stop assuming an outward expression that does not come from within you and is not representative of what you are in your inner being but is patterned after this age; but change your outward expression to one that comes from within and is representative of your inner being, by the renewing of your mind." [3]

If the first step in identifying yourself is to find out what you *care to do* and who you *care to be*, you must already know something about who you are in your inner being.

Finding out what you care to do hinges largely on your abilities and talents, your likes and dislikes. You are, of course, influenced by people you respect and admire. But hopefully you can decide according to what you really enjoy doing—what is personally satisfying to you.

This can be confusing—especially with other people constantly telling us what *they* want us to do. How can I know who I really am within my inner being?

Jesus promised, "When the Spirit of truth comes, he will guide you into all the truth" (John 16:13, RSV). It is the Holy Spirit who calls us to do a particular thing, who rescues us from going in a false direction, who leads us into the vocation and lifestyle that is most satisfying for us and the most helpful to other people.

My friend Marion has shared with me how her hus-

band Ken had trouble deciding whether God wanted
him to be a doctor or a minister. Finally he chose the
medical profession.

After the grueling years of medical school, internship,
and residency, he settled down to the life of a successful
pediatrician. In a very short time, he heard God's Spirit
urging him to give it up and go into the ministry. The
prospect was staggering! They had heavy obligations
and four small children.

They turned their backs on security, left their home,
and entered Southern Seminary. After seven more
years of study, Ken finished seminary with a doctorate
in Hebrew and biblical archaeology. Today he is a seminary professor. He practices pediatrics in a hospital
clinic on Thursday evenings and alternate Saturdays.
He ministers to adults in church through his Bible teaching. He is well respected by the Jewish community
through his lectures on Palestine and the Semitic lan-
guages. And during the summer months, he is an ar-
chaeologist in Israel, making a unique contribution to
biblical archaeology because of his background in medi-
cine. (Bones are an important item in archaeology!)

Here is one example of a person who was not bound
by the world's standard of success but was willing to
give it up. As a result, he knows a broader kind of
success. It is without the financial remuneration he
would have known in the medical profession, but it is
an expression of his inner being—as God revealed to
him the areas of his own potential.

What you "care to be" is a matter of character and
of personal preferences. What will your priorities in
life be? Do you want to be honest and open? Will you
be known as someone who is helpful and dependable?

Do you want to be intellectual? Had you rather be a bundle of fun? Do you want success at any price? Will you go after the fast buck? Is your deepest desire to be Christlike?

We have images thrown at us constantly. Be rich, be popular; be successful; be beautiful; be powerful. No wonder we're confused. Who is the real you? Who is that unique person in your inner being—that creation of God who dares to be different?

Each of us must arrive at our own identity if we want satisfaction and fulfillment. There are many factors which contribute to identity formation. Let me list some of them.

1. Identifying yourself means knowing how you look and how you feel. It means being aware of your assets, your abilities, your talents. It means accepting and liking yourself.

2. Knowing who you are includes arriving at a set of personal values—a personal code of conduct that is right for you. This creates a character that can be depended on.

3. Identifying yourself involves finding an occupation that is rewarding because it makes good use of a dominant ability. We have an innate desire to develop our abilities.

4. Finding your own identity means achieving an inner freedom from a group identity. All of us need some support from the group of people we identify with— our family, our church, our friends, our colleagues. But we can't agree with them at every point. We must know where our own personal identity begins; we must know how we are different from the group as a whole. How are you unique from your group?

5. Having an identity (knowing who you are) includes arriving at a philosophy of life (a religion, a faith) that holds life together. It means having some intelligent belief that gives meaning to life.

It seems to me that the Christian should be especially concerned about knowing who he is. We Christians are committed to Jesus Christ. This means we cannot be committed to the standards of the world. We are committed to finding out who we really are and being that authentic person in a personal relationship with Christ himself. In our friendship with Christ there are no pretenses, no attempts to impress, no fear of being misunderstood, no chance of being rejected.

Through this relationship we change our outward expression to one that corresponds to our inner being. According to Kenneth Wuest, this change comes when the Holy Spirit is "definitely and intelligently and habitually yielded to." We are given the courage to make that change, and we do it through a change in our thought processes. It is a "renewing" of the mind.

What a tremendous idea—having our thoughts made new again! No longer thinking as we've been conditioned to think in our superficial society. Shifting to a way of thinking that is uniquely our own, that corresponds to who we really are, and that fulfills our deepest needs. Thinking in union with God himself and in keeping with his plan for the universe!

T. B. Maston says, "We should have a deepening desire that our lives will increasingly express the same character traits found in God and that these traits will be the expression of a unified or integrated personality." [4]

After all we were created in the image of God. It's

natural that we feel the healthiest and most comfortable
inside when love, mercy, justice, faithfulness, and holi-
ness have settled (again) into our inner being. The potential for all of these qualities was there when we were
born. We lost them to a greater or lesser extent when
we departed from God's way.

Maston goes on to say, "To the degree that [these
traits] . . . become a part of the very essence of our
being, to that degree they will be the outer expressions
of a well-integrated personality." [5]

According to Paul, when our minds have been so renewed, we can truly test the will of God in our lives.
Some people are afraid of God's will. They are afraid
they won't like what they get. But when our minds
have been made new again by God's Spirit, we find
that his will "meets our specifications," and we "place
our approval on it."

Finding God's will for our lives means we do not
let the world around us "squeeze us into its own mould,"
(Rom. 12:2, Phillips). We do not have the same goals
as our materialistic society. We may not spend our time
and money in the frantic way the advertisers say we
should. We are free to choose a more sensible and meaningful way of life.

Here is the entire verse in Wuest's translation: "And
stop assuming an outward expression that does not
come from within you and is not representative of what
you are in your inner being but is patterned after this
age; but change your outward expression to one that
comes from within and is representative of your inner
being, by the renewing of your mind, resulting in your
putting to the test what is the will of God, the good
and well-pleasing and complete will, and having found

that it meets specifications, placing your approval upon it." [6]

[1] Erik H. Erikson, *Dimensions of a New Identity* (New York: W. W. Norton & Co., Inc., 1974), p. 124.
[2] Alexander Lowen, M.D., *The Betrayal of the Body* (New York: The Macmillan Company, 1967), pp. 3-5.
[3] From *The New Testament: An Expanded Translation* by Kenneth S. Wuest. © Copyright Wm. B. Eerdmans Publishing Company, 1961.
[4] T. B. Maston, *Why Live the Christian Life?* (Nashville: Thomas Nelson, Inc., 1974), p. 21.
[5] Ibid., p. 22.
[6] Wuest, op. cit.

To Think About and Do:

1. Were you conditioned to be a certain kind of person as you were growing up? Was your "conditioning" a positive or a negative experience?

2. Are there roles in life which you try to fulfill because someone else expects it of you?

3. One popular exercise to raise self-esteem is that of listing the things you like about yourself. If you do not already have such a list, start one. Add to it until you have at least ten items. Notice how many items on your list have to do with appearance and how many have to do with personality

4. List five of your favorite things to do. What does this list reflect about your personality?

To Read:

John Powell, *Why Am I Afraid to Tell You Who I Am?* (Niles, Illinois: Argus Communications, 1969).

Nelson Price, *How To Find Out Who You Are.* Nashville: Broadman Press, 1977.

Robert E. Ball, *The "I Feel" Formula.* Waco: Word Books, 1977.

14
On Not Thinking Too Highly of Yourself

Romans 12:3-8

In the last two years I have become more interested in the dynamics of getting along together as Christians. Although I really enjoy people, I also enjoy solitude. And when there has been a choice between the two, I've frequently opted for solitude. Heaven for me can be a quiet day at home or a calm evening with family.

But I have been more and more confronted with the New Testament emphasis on *koinonia*—being together in loving and supportive relationships.

I learned early in adolescence that I could survive without group support and that I usually preferred my own opinions to those of the group. At the same time I know I couldn't have survived without the love and support of a few people. And during that time in high school when I felt most isolated from a supportive small group, my large group at school "rescued" me by electing me to class positions.

It's important to be able to stand alone when necessary, but we need the love and support of other people in order to function as God meant for us to in the world.

In the twelfth chapter of Romans Paul gives some practical instructions for living together as Christians. In verses 3-8 he meets one primary problem head-on.

It is the problem of some people setting themselves up above others.

There is, of course, a place for healthy assertiveness. But it's a sign of insecurity to feel that we must always be the one who's "out in front."

We hear a lot of talk today about self-esteem. In *Hide or Seek*, James Dobson says there is an "epidemic of inferiority complexes." The experts agree that we should learn to think more highly of ourselves.

Yet, in Romans 12:3 Paul says, "Don't cherish exaggerated ideas of yourself or your importance" (Phillips). Paul was not implying that some people had overestimated their own worth. The price that Jesus paid for us leaves no doubt about each person's worth. The problem was in failing to recognize the worth of *everyone*. It was also in failing to be completely honest about their own growth.

At heart, we know that we aren't all we could be, and as a result we sometimes feel that other people don't appreciate us. We feel that we haven't received our fair share of recognition. We see others receiving acclaim, and we feel compelled to "get in on the act." There is the old saying, "If you don't toot your own horn, it may not get tooted!"

Apparently there were some people in the church in Rome like that. They felt it necessary to call attention to their own importance. Maybe some based their claim to superiority on being Jewish (that is, better than the Gentile Christians). Perhaps others were puffed up about their own spiritual gifts. One person may have been more intellectual, another person wealthier, than the others. Someone else was undoubtedly a better leader or teacher. Slaves or former slaves in the church may have been looked down on by the rest of the congregation.

Paul has a message for these people, and the message comes out of God's grace: "Don't cherish exaggerated ideas of yourself or your importance, but try to have a sane estimate of your capabilities" (Rom. 12:3, Phillips).

Let's get at the real issue. It isn't a matter of one person being more valuable than another. Each person is priceless. The real question is, how close have you come to being all that God wants you to be? How far have you progressed in reaching your full potential? Be honest in *that* estimate of yourself.

This quotation is from psychologist William Schutz in a book called *Joy: Expanding Human Awareness:* "If there is one statement true of every living person it must be this: he hasn't achieved his full potential. The latent abilities, hidden talents, and undeveloped capacities for excellence and pleasure are legion." [1]

The Christian life is to be a life of joy. There is little joy in a life that is unfulfilled—in which abilities are not developed and used, bodies are not appreciated, feelings are not expressed, love is not given and received. Luke 1:37 tells us that "With God nothing shall be impossible."

"The Impossible Dream" from *Man of La Mancha* expresses part of what it means to reach for your full potential.

What is your highest dream? What foe in your life needs to be fought? Have you dealt successfully with your sorrow? What good thing have you not dared to do? Is there wrong in your life that needs to be righted?

You can be better than you are.

On the other hand, Paul says, think sensibly, soberly, sanely about yourself. The danger in cherishing exaggerated ideas of your own importance lies in your forgetting the importance of other people. There is also the danger of being unrealistic about yourself. It's important to strive for your full potential, but it's also necessary to admit your limitations. Sometimes our limitations are set by our lack of confidence or lack of experience rather than by lack of ability. It's still better to recognize those limitations; they can be overcome in time.

Some people use their limitations as excuses. I remember a story by C. Roy Angel in *Iron Shoes* about a little man who was admiring a big strong man. The little man said, "If I were you, I'd go into the woods, find the biggest bear there, and tear him limb from limb!"

The big guy said, "There are plenty of little bears in the woods. Why don't you go kill one of them?"

"Try to have a sane estimate of your capabilities by the light of the faith that God has given to you all" (Rom. 12:3, Phillips). By faith, the Holy Spirit (the Spirit of truth) will reveal your true potential to you. Do you have the courage to recognize it? The more you exercise your faith, the more you can act on the potential God has revealed to you. Recognize it; use it; develop it, with God's help.

There lies latent deep within us a whole realm of abilities, talents, feelings, and capacities for love that are untapped. There are more personal resources than we can ever fully use in this lifetime. (After all, there is an eternity after this.)

Through our faith, the Holy Spirit will bring one or several of these latent abilities to our conscious attention. We will experience great happiness in developing and using this ability. Our knowledge and use of it is a gift of the Holy Spirit—otherwise we would never become aware of it. The Spirit breathes life into the "gift"; it becomes powerful and meaningful as we use it to help other people.

Paul reminds the Roman Christians that each of them has different gifts. Everyone's gift is important to the whole group; after all, we belong to each other (Rom. 12:5). The gift should be a source of joy, but not a source of pride. This is a fulfillment in our own time of God's promise to Abraham: "I will bless you so that you will be a blessing."

The gifts Paul lists here have to do with the Christian life in particular—helping and encouraging one another, speaking a word from God, teaching the faith, sharing with one another, leading the congregation, showing mercy and understanding. They are gifts which help us to support one another. We reach our greatest potential when we are a part of a supportive and loving group. This does not mean proving that you're more important or more capable than someone else. Rather, the joy comes from discovering you are more capable or more gifted than you realized you were. It's a joy to find you can be more than you ever dreamed of being. It's a matter of letting your outward expression represent all that you are in your own inner being.

"[God] by the power at work within us is able to do far more abundantly than all that we ask or think" (Eph. 3:20, RSV).

"I can do all things through Christ which strengthen-eth me" (Phil. 4:13, KJV).

---

[1] William Schutz, *Joy: Expanding Human Awareness* (New York: Grove Press, Inc., 1966), p. 15.

To Think About and Do:

1. What are your outstanding talents and abilities? Make a list of them. If you are in a group, get the opinions of other people.

2. Is there an ability you haven't developed which you'd like to work on?

3. Consider something definite you can do to develop your potential. Pray about it.

To Read:

Maurice Wagner, *The Sensation of Being Somebody.* Grand Rapids: Zondervan Publishing House, 1974.

Elizabeth O'Connor, *Eighth Day of Creation.* Waco: Word Books, 1971. About gifts and creativity.

15
Love Is What You Need

Romans 12:9-10; 13:8-10

The old gospel hymn says, "Love lifted me." In our society we're more likely to believe it's money, success, and prestige that have the power to lift us up and set us on the right course in life. We all do need recognition. Success and money bring one kind of recognition. But what about love? Without love we become emotionally and physically ill.

Love is the only key to getting along with one another in meaningful relationships. And this is what life is all about. The Christian life begins with a vital relationship to Jesus himself. It continues as that "love affair" includes more and more people who need love.

"Love must be completely sincere. . . . Love one another warmly as brothers in Christ, and be eager to show respect for one another" (Rom. 12:9-10, TEV).

The commandments . . . are summed up in the one command, "Love your fellow-man as yourself" (Rom. 13:9, TEV).

In his book, *Reality Therapy*, William Glasser says the two basic psychological needs of humans are: to love and be loved and to feel worthwhile to ourselves and others. Glasser goes on to say, "Essential to fulfilling our needs is a person, preferably a group of people, with whom we are emotionally involved" [1]

How terribly we limit the church when we fail to recognize that one of its most important functions (possibly *the* most important) should be to help meet these emotional needs for people. Everyone needs to experience the love of God in their lives. We all need to experience the love and acceptance of other people. Only then are we ready to get on with doing what is worthwhile.

Before he died, Jesus told his disciples, "You must love one another; I command you to love one another" (see John 15:12, 17). He could command this because he had put their needs before his own needs. He had demonstrated his love for them at the Supper; he was about to die for them. He was sending the Holy Spirit to comfort and help them. Now they must demonstrate their love for him by loving one another.

The church should be the setting in which we give and receive love; but one thing should be made clear at this point. People can't give what they have not received. We can't give love if we have never experienced it. Many people in the church have never actually known unconditional love. They need to be receivers. They can't be expected to give love until their own time of receiving has been satisfactory. And frequently those who need love the most are the most unlovely.

I remember a second-grade boy who attended our small Bible school one summer. He disrupted class so completely that he was sent out to the pastor to be dealt with. As the pastor spoke kindly to him, the boy started to cry. "I always get gypped," he sobbed. "I *always* get gypped."

He lived with his grandparents because his parents were divorced. He had looked forward to spending the summer with his mother. But at the last minute, she remarried and wrote that she couldn't take him. His reluctant grandparents were stuck with him.

This boy had never known real love; he had never known acceptance. He is a small example of the many people who come to our churches looking for something they have never had.

Most people who come to church don't express their needs openly. They are not like the couple who came to our church a few months ago and said simply, "We are here because we need the Lord." Instead, people come in various states of sophistication with most of their hurts carefully hidden.

Jesus could say to his disciples, "I command you to love one another," because they had known the warm love and acceptance of another person—Jesus himself. They could give out of their own overflowing cup without having to measure the return.

Love and acceptance can be experienced in the church through a person—preferably through a small group of persons. It can be a Sunday School class, a prayer group, a growth group, or simply a group of interested friends. We have to be known personally and intimately and feel loved before we're ready to love others.

Some people have an overwhelming sense of God's love when they first become a child of his. Usually the excitement and euphoria wear off after a period of time, and unless they have had an abundance of loving experiences growing up, they must begin learning what it means to love.

One powerful experience of the Christian life is that of loving and praising God with a larger group of people who are bound together in commitment to him. In such a service, love comforts, uplifts, and renews those who participate.

Why are we afraid to love?

My long-time friend has been a church member most of her life. She seldom attends church and has never been much involved. I have often heard her say, "I don't want everyone knowing my business." As a girl she was beautiful and talented. She is still a sensitive and compassionate person, but she doesn't want to get involved with other people.

Some of the people in her church would consider her a snob. But a few people know her on a deeper level. Her distant attitude covers up a deep sense of guilt. And she has paralyzing feelings of inferiority about not having developed her keen mind and her exceptional talents. Now her health is poor, and she depends heavily on drugs and alcohol.

In his book, *Why Am I Afraid to Love?* John Powell suggests that we fail in loving others because we are preoccupied with our own pain. Anxiety, guilt, and feelings of inferiority cause us so much discomfort that we can't reach out to others.

In a later book, *Why Am I Afraid to Tell You Who I Am?* Powell explains how love doesn't work because we are afraid to reveal ourselves to others. We're afraid they won't accept us if they really know us.

And in a third book, *The Secret of Staying in Love*, he suggests that the whole problem can be summed up in our lack of self-love. We can't love other people because we don't love ourselves. If we feel guilty and inferior we tend to think, "Why would anyone want my love? Why should anyone love me?" We can be expected to love our neighbor only to the extent that we can love ourselves.

In *The Art of Loving,* Erich Fromm suggests that we can learn to love (although it may be difficult) by practicing the basic elements in love. These elements are (in my own paraphrase):

1. *Care* and active concern for the life and growth of the other person.

2. *Response* to the needs (expressed or unexpressed) of that person.

3. *Respect* for the person as he is; being aware of his unique individuality and accepting that.

4. Truly *knowing* the other person; not a shallow knowledge, but a deep knowledge of his feelings and needs; experiencing some sense of union with that person. [2]

I used to know someone who was great at loving—but only at loving certain people. She heaped love, appreciation, and praises on those she admired. Other people—those she referred to as "losers"—received only tolerance or disdain. I found myself reacting toward this person with great dislike, even though she was loving toward me. How could I like such a strong personality who was so unfair? I could have sincerely "hit her over the head!"

All of us know how hard it is to love people we don't like. Pretending to love leaves us with an uneasy feeling. We haven't fooled ourselves or the other person. What are we to do?

We can *decide* to respect the other person; we can *decide* to be concerned. We can ask God to do good things for that person—while admitting in the prayer our own dislike. It has been my experience that if I persist in honest concern and prayers, the warm feelings will eventually follow. I will come to understand and accept the person in a loving way.

When there is a strong personality clash, the ones involved may have to "keep out of each other's hair" to some extent. Each person needs space to be himself. One responsibility of love is in respecting the other person's right to do things his own way.

All of us realize that we can do only so much loving. But there is a greater hope for us. C. H. Dodd, in his commentary on Romans ("The Moffatt New Testament Commentary," p. 197), says that "love is the supreme and all-inclusive gift of the Spirit." Thank goodness it doesn't all depend on us.

The Holy Spirit can do through us what we can't do ourselves. He can give us the courage to love. He can give us love for those who are "distant," those who are quarrelsome, those who "drive us up the wall." In all of our churches we must pray for the gift of love. It should be said of us, as it was said of the first-century Christians, "How they love one another!"

Paul observes that we should love one another with a family affection (Rom. 12:10). Members of a family share a natural bond of love. Those of us in God's family should have the warmest feelings of family affection; we've all been rescued by the same person. We should be delighted when someone else in our group is honored (just as a parent is delighted to have one of his children honored). As a matter of fact, we should "outdo one another in showing honor" (Rom. 12:10, RSV).

If our relationships are working right, we get a lot of pleasure out of honoring someone else. This is because we know that we and others in the group are also honored. We all have our moments of glory. We mutually honor and support one another. This is the Christian way of building self-esteem.

But keep it honest. Don't be a false "gusher." Give as much love as you can honestly give.

Many people get themselves heavily into debt and must always be occupied with trying to pay their debts. Paul says, "Don't owe any debts except the debt of love." Always be occupied with giving love to others. When the love of God is "poured into our hearts through the Holy Spirit" (Rom. 5:5, RSV), we can always be pouring love out to those who need it.

What a picture of the church—a place where we pour love out and receive love in return! A place where we are honored and where we honor others! I have heard it said of some churches, "As soon as you go in, you can feel the love!"

Pray for the gift of love. "In this life we have three lasting qualities—faith, hope and love. But the greatest of them is love" (1 Cor. 13:13, Phillips).

[1] William Glasser, *Reality Therapy: A New Approach to Psychiatry* (Lakeville, Connecticut: Institute of General Semantics, 1965), p. 8.

[2] See Erich Fromm, *The Art of Loving* (New York: Harper & Row Publishers, 1956), pp. 26-32.

To Think About and Do:

1. Are you a part of a small group which is supportive and loving? Is it a church group? If not, can you help to start a prayer, Bible study, or sharing group?

2. Recall a particularly encouraging or loving act of

someone (outside your family) toward you. How did you respond?

3. Think of someone you have difficulty liking. Begin to pray daily for that person.

To Read:

The book of 1 John is full of instructions about loving one another. Read it at one sitting.

John Powell, *The Secret of Staying in Love*. Niles, Illinois: Argus Communications, 1974.

16
How Much Are You Worth?

Romans 12:9,11

"Freud was once asked what he thought a normal person should be able to do well. The questioner probably expected a complicated, 'deep' answer. But Freud simply said, *Lieben und arbeiten* ('to love and to work')." [1]

Loving and working: Is this the essence of life? To a large extent it is. In the last chapter we talked about loving. In this chapter I'd like to approach more than the aspect of simply working. I'd like to get at the overall problem of being worth something to yourself and others. This is what your self-esteem hinges on. In order to feel worthwhile you must go further than finding something useful to do (work); you also must be a person of character—a person who "acts right."

We've discussed the problem of sin, but here I'd like to get at it from another angle. Let's be practical as well as spiritual.

I have been struck by the consensus among psychologists that in order to be a healthy personality, you must come to some decisions about right and wrong in your life.

. . . to be worthwhile, we must maintain a satisfactory standard of behavior.

. . . we must learn to correct ourselves when we do

wrong and to credit ourselves when we do right. If we do not evaluate our own behavior,

. . . act to improve our conduct where it is below our standards, we will not fulfill our need to be worthwhile and we will suffer as acutely as when we fail to love or be loved.[2] This is a statement from William Glasser, who has been so influential in the field of psychology in recent years. His opinion is shared by most other leading psychologists.

Paul's statement along these lines is quite succinct: "Hate what is evil; cling to what is good" (Rom. 12:9, NIV). We must love (cling to) what is good for us—what is right, what is constructive. We also should love what is good for other people—what is right, constructive, fair for them.

On the other hand, we should hate what is bad for ourselves and for others—whatever enslaves, destroys, or warps our growth; whatever causes harm or hurt; whatever separates us from God.

The mark of maturity is being able to tell the difference between good and evil. The Ten Commandments still provide a sturdy guideline, of course, but some of them can be interpreted in various ways. Does "Thou shalt not kill" mean you should not participate in war? Many Christians feel that it does.

The Commandment, "Thou shalt not commit adultery," is interpreted by some people to mean only that you must not be involved with another man's wife (since that is the literal meaning of the Hebrew word).

I will always remember the soul-searching I went through as a young person trying to determine right and wrong. My steady boyfriend was very much in love and wanted to get married. I knew that marriage was out of the question for me. As a college student I didn't as yet know who I was, much less whom I wanted to marry.

His proposal was, "If you won't marry me, at least give yourself to me—just once." I knew how much he needed love and reassurance. Considering the devotion he had shown to me over a period of years, it seemed like a small thing to ask.

But I believed that premarital sex was wrong for me. Two courses of action were open to me: (1) fulfill a deep desire for someone else (I was not without desire, of course)—or (2) tenaciously (and selfishly?) hold on to my own conviction. Which was the mature thing to do?

I could not tell what the long-range outcome would be—in terms of guilt, satisfaction, or fulfillment. I was sure it would involve guilt for me. Should I give up my principles to bring fulfillment to someone else—someone I felt a love and obligation toward?

My best judgment told me that if I agreed to a sexual union, it would be an emotionally binding experience for both of us. It would be much harder then to avoid marrying this person whose goals were not the same as mine.

I could resolve the dilemma because my ultimate commitment was to a higher person than my boyfriend. I was responsible to God himself and would have to trust him to take care of my friend.

The decision reinforced what I was already convinced of. Our relationship had gone on far too long; it was time to go our separate ways. A sexual union would be bad for me. I could not be responsible for him.

Until we decide what is right in our own lives and

abide by that, we can't do much about what is right
or wrong for the world. Of course, we can't impose
our personal standards of conduct on everyone else.
They have a right to make their own decisions.

Some Christians argue that the Bible gives clear guidance about right and wrong. I believe that it does. But
those of us who "inherited" the Christian code of conduct from our parents come to a time when we must
decide for ourselves, "This is right for me." That is a
part of deciding "who you care to be," as Erikson
phrases it.

There are many areas of evil in the world. Prejudice,
human enslavement, sexual exploitation, poverty, and
disease are a few of these. The Christian is engaged
in a war against evil. "Hate what is evil; cling to what
is good." Here the struggle moves beyond our own personal lives to involvement with the struggle of other
people. The outcome of having a "renewed mind" is
right thought—which leads to right action. But it must
begin on a very personal level—in your own life, with
your own private actions.

Another aspect of feeling worthwhile has to do with
work. According to Erikson, your occupation should involve the use of a "dominant faculty"—one of your
own outstanding abilities. If you are involved in such
an occupation, it brings you a sense of satisfaction. It
challenges you. You really enjoy the work. You are
pleased with the place it gives you in life; you feel good
about the contribution it allows you to make to the
world; you benefit from the people you are associated
with. If your occupation meets these criteria, you feel
worthwhile to yourself and to other people.

For the Christian, there is also the spiritual dimension

that requires us to ask: Is God pleased with what I am doing? Can I serve him in this occupation? Is this what he wants me to do in the world?

Proverbs 31 gives a beautiful description of a woman who is involved in a challenging occupation. Managing her home is an important part of her work, but she lives her life as an astute business person. Read the entire passage in Proverbs 31:10-31 to fully appreciate it. Notice particularly these clauses:

—She seeks wool and flax, and works with willing hands.

—She considers a field and buys it; with the fruit of her hands she plants a vineyard.

—She perceives that her merchandise is profitable.

—She opens her hand to the poor, and reaches out her hands to the needy.

—She makes linen garments and sells them; she delivers girdles to the merchants.

—Strength and dignity are her clothing, and she laughs at the time to come.

—Her children rise up and call her blessed; her husband also, and he praises her.

—. . . a woman who fears the Lord is to be praised.

Here is a person who is "doing her thing." She cares for her family (and for the poor), but notice that, unlike some working wives, she is not expected to do all the housework as well. She has a staff of servants (maidens) which she manages (v. 15)! Her business is profitable. She is admired and appreciated by her family.

A glance at the description in Proverbs 31 will tell you that this person likes herself and likes what she is doing. Anyone with a challenging and worthwhile occupation reaps the same benefits in terms of physical and emotional well-being.

In Romans 12:11 Paul says, "Work hard, and do not be lazy. Serve the Lord with a heart full of devotion" (TEV).

The RSV puts it this way: "Never flag in zeal, be aglow with the Spirit, serve the Lord."

Whatever our occupation, we Christians should be aware that we're working for good in the world (and in our own families); we're working against evil.

Be aglow with the Spirit!

[1] Erik H. Erikson, *Identity: Youth and Crisis* (New York: W. W. Norton and Company Inc., 1968), p. 136.

[2] William Glasser, op. cit., pp. 10-11.

To Think About and Do:

1. How do you come to a decision about right and wrong? Does the Bible give you practical help? If so, how?

2. Are your abilities put to good use in your occupation? If not, do you develop them in other ways?

3. Are you conscious of serving other people through your secular vocation?

4. How do you serve the Lord in your life? Does this also involve your vocation?

To Read:

T. B. Maston, *Why Live the Christian Life?* Nashville: Thomas Nelson, Inc., 1974.

17
Happiness Is a Person

Romans 12:12-13

Sometimes the people who have every apparent reason to be happy are the unhappiest. Linda is such a person. She has beautiful children, a devoted husband, a lovely home. She is slender, attractive, sensitive, and intelligent. Her husband's income is above average among professional vocations.

But Linda suffers from chronic depression. It's a common story in our time. I know the reasons Linda gives for being depressed—an unhappy childhood, an inability to relate to others, a feeling of having failed in job opportunities, deep-seated feelings of inferiority.

Professional counseling has helped Linda to understand herself. Medication has helped her to continue functioning, but the depression persists.

I am well aware of the futility of offering religious clichés to this friend. Too many people have already said, "Pray about it; cheer up; trust the Lord." These are people who do not understand depression and who certainly don't understand Linda.

Paul offers a prescription in Romans 12:12-13 which I believe is good solid advice for the Christian when life is looking grim. The words themselves are not a panacea, but the experience they suggest offers peace and stability. The words probably would not help Linda, but if she could experience what Paul is talking about, courage and optimism would surely begin to enter her life.

"Base your happiness on your hope in Christ" (Rom. 12:12, Phillips).

Most of us know how unstable our emotions can be. The hint of criticism, the feeling of failure, the sting of rejection, a disappointment—any of these can give us a feeling of despondency. Illness, injury, disability, financial disaster, the loss of a loved one, the threat of death—all are real reasons for life to look dark and hopeless.

When I was in college, it was common for the "thinking" Christians to make light of those who praised the Lord when the "roof was falling in." The implication was that those who automatically praised the Lord in the face of disaster never realized the full extent of what was going on. Perhaps there was some truth in that criticism.

On the other hand, what if you realize the disaster, feel the despair, and still see reasons to be thankful? What if you believe God wants to bring peace and help into the situation? That kind of assurance is based on our hope in Christ.

We talked about hope in chapter 7. Christian hope is not a naive wishing for good to happen. It is a firm expectation based on what God has done in the past (as recorded in the history of the people of Israel, in the sending of Jesus, in the resurrection) and on what he has promised for the future. It's also more than a general belief that in the end God will do what's right for mankind.

Our personal Christian hope comes out of our intimate friendship with Christ. It is the result of what the Holy Spirit has already done in our personal lives. It is the firm assurance that God will do for us all that needs to be done. The RSV says, "Rejoice in your hope" (Rom. 12:12).

When we live with the steady hope that God is good, that he plans good things for us, and that he wants us to experience the best in our lives, we have reason for peace and happiness. We have courage to face whatever the day may bring.

"When trials come, endure them patiently" (Rom. 12:12, Phillips).

Like the first statement, this one is easier said than done.

I know a Christian girl who married a capable and intelligent young man. Although he was a Christian, he was very unstable. During their two years of marriage, he frequently changed his mind about what vocation he wanted to enter, which degree he would finish, and—worst of all—whether he should have married at all.

According to Wuest's commentary, the Greek word for "patient" means to remain under. This means not seeking to escape the hardship but eager to learn the lessons it can teach.

My friend remained in the marriage patiently (and hopefully), went through the counseling faithfully, encouraged her husband as much as she could. The lessons were painful; the pressures and distress were great. But when her husband left her for the last time, she knew she could go on without him. She knew she could begin again, a wiser person and more sensitive to God's leadership in her life.

The word translated "trials" means pressure, oppression, affliction, tribulation, distress.

. To endure trials, or to remain under pressure implies a passive stance. If you've been "tried," you know it involves more than passivity. There are positive actions to take. Encouraging yourself to "rejoice in hope" is a positive action. Another positive action is prayer. *The New English Bible* translates this part of the verse, "Persist in prayer" (Rom. 12:12, NEB).

Many of you who've been through crises in your lives could testify to the power of prayer at such times. Prayer has multiple benefits. It sustains the praying person; it gives that person something positive to do; and it acts as a force to bring help and healing into the situation.

I was all the way across the United States when my sister and niece were in an automobile accident. My seven-year-old niece was killed instantly; my sister was in critical condition. It would take all night for my husband and me to fly home. What could I do but pray?

While my husband went to the bank for money, I began to pack and as I packed I fell down by the bedside begging God to spare my sister's life. She had a husband and another child to care for.

Throughout the night on the plane I continued to pray. Toward morning I began to feel some peace, some assurance that things would turn out well.

My sister lived. I think I would have experienced the same peace at that time even if she had not lived. The assurance was in knowing that God had heard my prayer, that he was aware of the situation, that he would not leave us without help.

The crisis concerning my sister's life lasted only three

or four days. The crisis of their adjustment following the accident was much longer. Some times of hardship last weeks, months—even years. Throughout this time the Christian has hope: God is alive and well. There is something strategic to be done—pray at all times. (There may be, of course, many other important things to be done, but prayer should accompany all of them.)

"Base your happiness on your hope in Christ. When trials come endure them patiently; steadfastly maintain the habit of prayer" (Rom. 12:12, Phillips).

This is good advice not only in times of crisis, hardship, or depression; each day brings it's own problems and pressures.

I would like to suggest one other practice which gives the Christian life a real lift. Paul includes it as another practical action for the Christian to take. He mentioned it first in verse 8: "Let the man who is called to give, give freely" (Phillips). Now in verse 13 he says,

"Give freely to fellow-Christians in want." *The New International Version* reads. "Share with God's people who are in need."ʼ

With our economy as it is today, we might easily feel that we can't afford to give much to the church or to needy people. Sometimes it's downright discouraging to find that we're required to spend so much for shelter, food, and clothes; there's seldom anything left over to give.

Erich Fromm makes an interesting observation about giving. "In the sphere of material things giving means being rich. Not he who *has* much is rich, but he who *gives* much. The hoarder who is anxiously worried about losing something is . . . the poor, impoverished man, regardless of how much he has. Whoever is capable of giving of himself is rich." [1]

A chance to be rich. There is a prospect which is open to all people—especially Christians. We have a rich Father; we can participate in his riches by giving.

Christian opinions vary about giving. Some insist that the more you give the more you get (see Luke 6:38). All of us would surely agree that when we share with someone we don't expect that person to pay us back. We *can* expect that the heavenly Father will continue to provide for our needs. He has an inexhaustible supply. Giving then becomes an expression of faith. It colors all of life with optimism.

Erich Fromm says, "He [who gives] does not give in order to receive; giving is in itself exquisite joy." [2]

---

[1] Erich Fromm *The Art of Loving* (New York: Harper & Row Publishers, 1956), p. 24.
[2] Ibid., p. 25.

To Think About and Do:

1. What is your happiness based on—circumstances, money, somebody? Is our Lord a real person to you? Is he important enough to control your happiness?

2. One of my favorite devotional books advises, "When you face a real need, look around for something to give away." How do you interpret that statement? Do you agree or disagree?

3. Recall an especially difficult time in your life. What sustained you?

To Read:

William Parker and Elaine St. Johns, *Prayer Can Change Your Life*. New York: Cornerstone Library, 1974.

A. J. Russell, ed., *God Calling*. Old Tappan, New Jersey: Fleming H. Revell Company, 1972.

18
Talk About a Beautiful Body

Romans 12:13-16

The most beautiful body in the world should be the "body of believers." I mean, of course, those persons who make up the body of Christ in the world. We are the ones who must live out the words which Jesus claimed: "The Spirit of the Lord is upon me" (Luke 4:18, RSV).

Our responsibility is to the poor, the captive, the blind, and the oppressed—whether these conditions are spiritual or physical. We are responsible for these persons when they are within the body of believers or outside it in the world.

In his book, *A Place for You,* Paul Tournier talks about the importance of each person having a place of his own in life. Most of us know what it means to get attached to a house, a plot of ground, a neighborhood. These places give us a sense of identity, of belonging. As a small child it's important to have a secure place in some sort of family—a place where we're loved. Later we find a place in school, with a peer group, and further along, with friends and colleagues.

Dr. Tournier notes that once we have had a secure place in life, we can always thereafter find a place for ourselves in the world. But the person who has never had a real place (with loving people) will always have difficulty fitting in comfortably with any group of people. He will continue to feel that he doesn't belong.

Each person needs to know he is accepted and approved by other persons in order to feel "at home." If a Christian is to grow and develop, he must find a secure place with a group of other Christians.

An unprecedented number of American families change their residence each year. As a result, we have a large number of Americans who feel very much displaced. They are away from familiar surroundings, away from family ties, and away from the support of friends and acquaintances. The stress of severing close relationships and leaving the familiar behind takes a heavier emotional toll than might be expected.

Paul's advice to the church in Rome is especially good advice to churches in our society today. The Christians there were living in a time of stress. Many of them had severed ties with friends and relatives in order to join the Christian community. They were an unpopular minority. Persecution was possible; alienation was common. It was especially important that the church should be a family.

We've already considered Paul's words about family affection in the church: "Be devoted to one another in brotherly love" (Rom. 12:10, NIV), and his advice about sharing: "Share with God's people who are in need" (v. 13, NIV). He has several other words of instruction about being supportive and getting along together in the Christian family. The next of these is also in verse 13: "Practice hospitality" (RSV).

Recently in a small group, Toni shared with us her feelings about having moved frequently during her married life. She and her husband have lived in many different places both in and out of the continental United States. During part of this time they weren't Christians.

"I can't believe how much easier it is when you're a Christian," she said. "Now the first thing we do when we move is find a church of our choice. Immediately we feel at home. We know that whatever we need, we can call on the people at church. They make sure that we're taken care of."

That's what Paul was talking about—share food, share time, share support, share love with those who need it. And look for opportunities to have people in your home.

It's easy to get into the habit of having the same friends over time after time knowing that they, in turn, will offer you their hospitality. But we must remember to include the ones who don't yet have friends, who are hungry for fellowship, and also those who may not be able to repay the favor.

It is especially meaningful to be hospitable to strangers—that is, to those who are new in the area or in the church. Jesus spoke some rather ominous words in this regard: "I was a stranger but you would not welcome me in your homes" (Matt. 25:43, TEV). Obviously we can't entertain every new family we meet. But each family needs to know two or three other families in the church on a personal basis.

When my son was three years old, he attended nursery school two mornings a week. After several weeks his teacher mentioned to me that he would not play with anyone in his class. I was quite surprised, and when I questioned him about this he said very seriously, "Mom, they don't have houses."

I understood what he meant. All his other playmates

were friends whose homes he visited. He was familiar with their houses, their toys, their families. He could not relate to children whose only place seemed to be at nursery school. They were strange children without houses.

All of us know the importance of having personal friends who will share our joys and sorrows. In verse 15 Paul says, "Rejoice with those who rejoice, weep with those who weep" (RSV). Joy is so much more joyful when you share it. And sorrow is not quite so heavy when shared.

My husband Glenn and I will always feel a closeness to friends with whom we have shared grief. Some of them live far away, and we have lost direct contact; but a bond of understanding remains because we have shared their sorrow.

Too often our churches are cold places as far as emotion is concerned. Dr. Paul Tournier is a dedicated Christian psychiatrist. He makes this observation (concerning psychiatric patients): "It is often very difficult for a patient who has been cured, or at least undergone an improvement in his condition, to feel at home in the church, even if he wants to. He finds it so impersonal, so cold and conventional after the stirring experiences he has had in the psychotherapist's consulting room."[1]

This shouldn't be true. A church can't be a truly loving group of people if there is no sharing of joy, of sorrow, of concerns. I want to worship with people who are sensible and stable, but I also want to be with people who *feel* things—and who are not afraid to share their feelings.

Another mark of a loving Christian group is the feeling of harmony. Paul says simply,

"Live in harmony with one another" (Rom. 12:16, RSV). This is a characteristic of love—a feeling of unity. When we love someone, we enter into that person's feelings. We share thoughts because we want to understand one another. Dedication to Christ and love as a gift of the Spirit, can bring about unanimity even in a large church family. Each person then shares the mind of Christ (see Phil. 2). This does not mean that everyone will always have the same opinion (as we shall see in Rom. 14 and 15). There is always room for diversity of opinion, but we remain united in Spirit and in purpose.

Paul has two additional words of instruction in verse 16. First, "Don't become snobbish but take a real interest in ordinary people" (Phillips). This is reminiscent of something Paul says in the first chapter of Romans: "For I have an obligation to all peoples, to the civilized and to the savage, to the educated and to the ignorant" (Rom. 1:14, TEV). Everyone needs the love and acceptance of other people. We should remember Jesus' concern for ordinary people. He was unimpressed by important people and impressive surroundings. He was concerned about the basic needs of persons—regardless of their prestige or wealth.

Paul's other word in verse 16 is,

"Don't become set in your own opinions" (Phillips), and *The Living Bible* says, "And don't think you know it all!"

This is a good word of advice to those of us who have been in the church a long time. Some of us begin to think we know all there is to know about how to run a church, about doctrine, about education, about music. And there are always a few people who won't let others have their own opinion.

I remember a fine Christian man who was very opinionated. He usually spoke as if he had the final word on whatever was being discussed. He intimidated some people, he made a few others furious, and quite a few more reacted with dislike. Those who got to know him on a personal basis, however, were surprised to find that he was a compassionate and helpful friend. He could have been so much more effective as a Christian leader if he hadn't come across as a know-it-all.

The main concern here, of course, is not how we "come across." The question is whether we are sensitive to the feelings and opinions of other people. That sensitivity is another mark of love and maturity.

[1] Paul Tournier, *A Place for You* (New York: Harper & Row, Publishers, 1966), p. 79.

To Think About and Do:

1. Do you fit in easily with new people and new situations? Can you tell why or why not?

2. What makes you feel most welcome when you move to a new community? Do you do the same for new people that you know of?

3. Are there good opportunities for people to make friends in your church? What can you do to help?

4. What kind of feelings are you aware of during worship at your church? Pray that your church will be warm and receptive.

To Read:

Karen Burton Mains, *Open Heart, Open Home.* Elgin, Illinois: David C. Cook Publishing Co., 1976. (How to find joy through sharing your home with others.)

John Claypool, *Tracks of a Fellow Struggler.* Waco: Word Books, 1974. (How to handle grief.)

19
Loving in an Unfriendly World

Romans 12:14,17-21; 13

A common message in our day is, "Live in the now." It means don't spend time fretting over the past, and don't invest everything in planning for the future. Live now. The past is gone; there may not be a future.

This is good advice. Of course, at times the past must be dealt with; and it's wise to give some thought to the future. As Christians, we know we do have a future. We just don't know how much of it will be spent on earth.

One of the common themes of the Bible concerns the temporary aspect of our time in this world. The Old Testament points frequently to the brevity of a person's life span. The New Testament adds to that the immanence of Christ's return. This adds up to a concise message: Live wisely. Be ready.

One aspect of living wisely is the task of relating wisely to the present world—the "now" that is all around us. If it's a friendly world, enjoy it. If it's a hostile world, approach it lovingly and positively.

It is helpful to remember what was happening in Rome when Paul wrote this letter to the beautiful body of Christians there. At this time (the A.D. 50's), Christians were not yet being persecuted by the Roman government. Within the next decade, however, Nero would outlaw Christianity, and widespread persecution would be common.

At the time of Paul's letter, Christians did meet with persecution in Rome, but it was by pagans and non-Christian Jews rather than by the government. Although it was still legal to be a Christian, it certainly was not popular to be one. Christians were viewed with skepticism and suspicion.

Jews had been banished from Rome in A.D. 49, but allowed to return later. Rioting was cited as the reason for their banishment.

You can see how important it was for the Roman Christians to live above criticism. Paul gives them some practical advice. It concerns how to respond to those who mistreat you, and how to live so that you will be respected in a non-Christian world. "Ask God to bless those who persecute you; yes, ask him to bless, not to curse . . . . If someone does evil to you, do not pay him back with evil. Try to do what all men consider to be good. Do everything possible, on your part, to live at peace with all men. Never take revenge, my friends" (Rom. 12:14,17-19, TEV).

You can see that love is to be the outstanding characteristic of the Christian. This holds true outside the church just as much as it does within the church.

We are not likely to be openly persecuted today because we are Christians, but we may very likely meet with hostility because of our Christian stand or our Christian life-style. The Holy Spirit works through Christ's followers to convict the world of sin, and many people will resent that.

Christians are humans, and when we meet with hostility and dislike it is natural to feel dislike and to give hostility in return. Paul warns against that. "Ask God to bless those who persecute you" (v. 14, TEV). This is reminiscent of Jesus' words in Matthew 5:43-47.

"You have heard that it was said, 'Love your friends, hate your enemies.' But now I tell you: love your enemies, and pray for those who persecute you, so that you will become the sons of your Father in heaven. For he makes his sun to shine on bad and good people alike, and gives rain to those who do good and those who do evil. Why should God reward you if you love only the people who love you? Even the tax collectors do that! And if you speak only to your friends, have you done anything out of the ordinary?" (TEV).

We've heard "love your enemy" so long that we're likely to forget to do it. After all, it doesn't sound very practical. We need to have it underlined: *When someone mistreats you, ask God to be good to that person.* This is the sodium bicarbonate that neutralizes the acid of hatred.

It should be obvious to other people that you are a *good* person, that you want to live at peace, and that you have no desire to get revenge (see Rom. 12:17-19). "Instead, as the scripture says: 'If your enemy is hungry, feed him; if he is thirsty, give him to drink; for by doing this you will heap burning coals on his head.' Do not let evil defeat you; instead, conquer evil with good" (Rom. 12:20-21, TEV).

Here is a chance to be creative. What does your enemy really need that you can give him? How can you help him out in some ordinary way, as you would help a friend? What practical thing can you do for him—graciously, with no strings attached?

C. H. Dodd reminds us that evil can never be overcome by evil, but only by a greater good.

"The Spirit of the Lord is upon me,
   because he has chosen me to preach the good news
      to the poor.
He has sent me to proclaim liberty to the captives,
   and recovery of sight to the blind;
to set free the oppressed,
   and announce that the time has come
when the Lord will save his people" (Luke
      4:18-19, TEV).

What if the poor person, the captive, the blind man, the victim of oppression, is your enemy? What if he is in all of these conditions spiritually? Can you allow God to love him through you? That's the most positive way to overcome evil with good.

There are many non-Christians in my small neighborhood. Some of them I'm just getting acquainted with. I'm not aware of any who are poor, blind, or oppressed. And I don't feel that any one of them is an enemy. Most of those I know are friendly and gracious. But there are some who have a low opinion of evangelical Christians. I also know that in this affluent county where the rate of alcoholism, divorce, and suicide is very high there are those in my own community too who are spiritually and emotionally oppressed, blind, and poor. My responsibility here is to share love—just as it would be if I lived among those who were physically oppressed. I can find opportunities to get acquainted through school and community activities. I can pray for my community and my neighbors. I can ask God for opportunities to help those who need help.

Paul's next instruction to Christians in a non-Christian world is: be responsible, law-abiding citizens. Read Romans 13. In it Paul reminds Roman Christians to keep the laws of the land, pay taxes and dues honestly, and show respect for law and government officials.

The Roman government was at this time protecting rather than persecuting Christians. Paul urges Christ's followers to cooperate with the government and support it. Governments are God's way of keeping peace and order in a country. Even when government officials go astray and bring evil to the land (as Nero would soon do in Rome), Christians are to respect the government as God's institution and pray for right and justice to be administered there again (see 1 Tim. 2:1-2; 1 Pet. 2:13-17.) This is a good reminder for us to support our own government and pray for its leaders. Those of us who live in a democratic society have the additional responsibility of seeing that the right leaders are elected and the proper laws are passed.

Another Christian responsibility is that of paying our debts—financial obligations and debts of love. Too many Christians (as a matter of fact, too many Christian leaders), are negligent about paying their debts. Poor money management no doubt accounts for most of this. Jesus said that in relating to the world, we are to be "wise as serpents and harmless as doves" (Matt. 10:16, KJV). Here is Paul's advice:

"Be in debt to no one—the only debt you should have is to love one another. Whoever loves his fellow-man has obeyed the Law . . . . Whoever loves his fellow-man will never do him wrong. To love, then, is to obey the whole Law" (Rom. 13:8,10, TEV).

If you owe money, pay it; be dependable. And always

be dependable about giving love.

The Roman Christians were probably tempted at times to revert back to their pagan ways. Paul uses the reminder of Christ's return as a strong incentive for them to stick to the Christian way of life.

"You know what hour it is: the time has come for you to wake up from your sleep. For the moment when we will be saved is closer now than it was when we first believed . . . . Let us conduct ourselves properly, as people who live in the light of day; no orgies or drunkenness, no immorality or indecency, no fighting or jealousy. But take up the weapons of the Lord Jesus Christ, and stop giving attention to your sinful nature, to satisfy its desires" (Rom. 13:11,13-14, TEV).

Drunkenness, fighting, indecency, immorality—these are ways to wreck the Christian life and ruin a Christian testimony. Love, self-esteem, being worthwhile to others should help eliminate that kind of living. Paul's advice is simple: "Clothe yourselves with the Lord Jesus Christ" (13:14, NIV).

To Think About and Do:

1. Who are your enemies? Are they also friends or relatives? Is an enemy anyone toward whom you feel hostility?

2. Who are the people who might consider you an enemy? What can you do about it?

3. Do you set a Christian example in observance of laws? In your money management?

4. List ways you can show love to those in your neighborhood.

20
Learning to Take Care

Romans 14; 15:1-7

I remember as a young person out on my own feeling very strongly that I was accountable only to God. That conviction gave me all the freedom I could handle and all the guidelines I needed. There were other people, of course, to be taken into consideration. But the big question was a matter of deciding what God had to say about it. If I really had his guidance, I thought I didn't have to worry about the affect on other people. With God's help, I was capable of taking care of myself; surely they could do the same.

But how are we Christians to behave toward one another when we disagree about what is right and wrong? Such disagreement is common, of course. When I was young it had to do with dancing, going to the drive-in, and what you could do on Sunday. In some churches it concerned make-up, jewelry, and the length of dresses.

Today it's more likely to involve social drinking and sexual behavior, or speaking in tongues and faith healing. Or perhaps it involves how the Christian should spend his money.

What are the areas of disagreement in your Christian group? What do you think Paul would say about such questions?

In Paul's day the issues were commonly (1) the observance of the sabbath and other Jewish religious days, (2) the eating of meat that had been consecrated to a false god, and (3) whether a Christian was better off being a vegetarian, because God had given specific Old Testament regulations regarding "unclean" meat.

Many Jewish Christians felt obligated to please God by keeping the old holy day and meat-eating regulations. And any sensitive Christian might feel spiritually contaminated if he ate meat that had been dedicated to another god! Such meat was commonly sold in the marketplace.

Paul gives some solid guidelines. First of all, be sure of your own convictions. Develop them with the knowledge that you belong to the Lord. "If we live, we live for the Lord; and if we die, we die for the Lord. Whether therefore we live or die, we belong to the Lord" (Rom. 14:8, NEB).

We feel very strongly about our convictions if they are genuine—and rightly so. After all, our attitudes toward right and wrong drastically affect our relationship to God himself. No wonder we get upset when someone makes light of our stand. Strong differences of opinion about such religious matters can split a church.

Paul gave his own view about the issues he mentioned: Christians who felt obligated to follow Jewish rules, and Christians who were intimidated by idols were still weak in the faith. Those who lived free of Jewish rules and those who could "hoot" at idols were more secure in their faith.

You can see that more is involved than simply coming to a sincere conviction—even when we feel that the

Holy Spirit has guided our thinking. Other people are just as sincere about their conviction. Are we to say that the Holy Spirit has not guided them?

No. Paul urges us to respect the other person's opinion. Some people are at a stage of moral development that requires adherence to rules—just as children need firm rules until they are old enough to manage responsibly without such restraints. More mature Christians develop a knowledge of God's nature through studying the Scripture and a sensitivity to the Spirit's leadership which allows them to live freely without any rules except the rule of love (Rom. 13:8-10).

Obviously, the more mature Christian is the one who should shoulder the responsibility of keeping peace when there are differing convictions.

Am I implying that anyone's conviction is OK as long as it is sincere? No, I definitely am not. Some tragic mistakes have been made by people who thought they were doing right. Deciding about right and wrong is serious business. It's one of those things that requires an eye on the future: "How will this action affect my tomorrows?"

Erik Erikson says once we have passed adolescence (having decided what we *care to do* and who we *care to be*) we will decide whom we *care to be with*. Normally, Christians choose to spend much of their time with other Christians. Beyond that we decide what and whom we can *take care of*. This means deciding what you can do to make the world a better place. For the Christian, it includes deciding what we can do to make the church a better place and what we can do to take care of her people. It means putting the kingdom of God first in our lives.

Paul gives us an important reminder. He says the Kingdom of God is not about rules and regulations, but about "righteousness and peace and joy in the Holy Spirit" (Rom. 14:17, RSV). He goes on to say, "Let us then pursue what makes for peace and for mutual up-building" (Rom. 14:19, RSV).

What can we do to help bring about peace in the church? What can we do to "build up" other Christians?

1. Determine not to argue with others about their convictions.

"If a man is weak in his faith you must accept him without attempting to settle doubtful points" (Rom. 14:1, NEB).

2. If someone believes in doing something which you think is wrong, don't get upset with him; don't pass judgment on him. He is accountable to God and not to you.

"Who are you to pass judgement on someone else's servant? Whether he stands or falls is his own Master's business; and stand he will, because his Master has power to enable him to stand" (14:4, NEB).

3. Don't look down your nose or be contemptuous of another Christian because you feel he is unenlightened. Instead, respect the person by respecting his opinion—even if it is narrow and legalistic. Remember that he is God's weak child. Deal gently with him.

"Why, then, do you criticize your brother's actions, why do you try to make him look small?" (Rom. 14:10, Phillips).

4. Don't openly practice what you believe is right if others believe it is wrong. There are two reasons for this: It may cause you to be unjustly criticized.

"Do not let your good be spoken of as evil" (Rom. 14:16, RSV).

"What for you is a good thing must not become an occasion for slanderous talk" (Rom. 14:16, NEB).

It could upset the faith of a weak Christian. "Do not, for the sake of food, destroy the work of God. . . . it is right not to eat meat or drink wine or do anything that makes your brother stumble" (Rom. 14:20,21, RSV).

5. Let your personal convictions be between yourself and God. Enjoy what you believe is right for you whenever the situation allows it.

"So whatever you believe about these things keep between yourself and God. Blessed is the man who does not condemn himself by what he approves" (Rom. 14:22, NIV).

6. Don't let someone else talk you into doing what you think is wrong. If you do, you are asking for trouble.

"But a man who has doubts is guilty if he eats, because his action does not arise from his conviction, and anything which does not arise from conviction is sin" (Rom. 14:23, NEB).

I might sum all of this up by saying, arrive at your own convictions through prayer, Scripture, and other kinds of study. Feel confident that between you and God things are right, and that your conviction is the proper one for you to hold. You may want to hear a variety of Christian opinions before deciding.

Allow others to have their own opinion. Be sensitive to their belief. Don't get upset when they differ from you. Relate to them with genuine respect and love.

We hear a lot about assertiveness these days. Classes are being offered in assertiveness training. Many people in our world today have never dared to be assertive. Some children are not allowed to voice an individual opinion. They cannot express their feelings (anger or dislike, for example) without the threat of punishment.

Some women have never learned to make a decision on their own. They have moved from the dominance of parents to the dominance of a husband. It's imperative for the sake of mental health, that each person be able to make a decision or reach an opinion without fear of being "put down." Self-respect as well as self-confidence is at stake. If the church is to be a place where everyone is accepted, then we cannot afford to squelch one another.

Those of us who are more mature in the faith should feel secure enough to give up an opinion now and then or to sacrifice an enjoyment for someone else's spiritual welfare.

We usually think of sacrifice as something that must be given up reluctantly or as a hardship that is imposed upon us. It is healthier (and more correct) to think of a sacrifice as something we offer to God out of love. In that case, it results in joy rather than resentment. The right kind of sacrifices enrich our lives.

"Whom do you *care to be with?*" Whom can you *take care of?*" Jesus spent much of his time with persons who understood him and who shared his goals. He spent even more time with those who needed his help. These are the persons for the Christian, too. We *enjoy* the people who understand us and who share our goals. We want to be with them. We *need* to be helpful to people who need our help—the weak, the confused, the downtrodden. We can help *take care of* them.

When all of us are living in harmony, we glorify God.

"May the God of steadfastness and encouragement grant you to live in such harmony with one another, in accord with Christ Jesus, that together you may with one voice glorify the God and Father of our Lord Jesus Christ. Welcome one another, therefore, as Christ has welcomed you, for the glory of God" (Rom. 15:5-7, RSV).

Take care! [1]

---

[1] I am indebted to Erik H. Erikson, *Dimensions of a New Identity* (New York: W. W. Norton and Co., Inc., 1974), p. 124, for the take-care idea.

To Think About and Do:

1. Do you consider yourself to be strong enough as a Christian and as a person to care for the spiritual needs of weaker Christians?

2. Can you be assertive when you need to be for your own welfare? Can you say a firm but gentle no to those who demand too much?

3. Who take care of your emotional and spiritual needs when you need help? (All of us need a friend like that!)

4. Does it threaten you when other people challenge your convictions? How can you become more secure?

To Read:

Paul Tournier, *A Place for You.* New York: Harper & Row, 1966.

21
What Are You Doing Here?

Romans 15:22 to 16:27

At some point, most of us seriously face the question, What am I doing here? Am I doing what I was created to do? Is there more to life than I have discovered?

The apostle Paul is a good example of a person who was living a fulfilled life. He loved what he was doing, and he never tired of making plans for the future.

Paul was a changed man after being confronted by the great Light—Jesus of Nazareth. Paul had asked Jesus the question, "What will you have me do?" From that moment the kingdom of God moved into first place in his life. The persecutor became the lover. His life took on a different meaning.

How was this carried out? First of all, after Paul met Jesus he took time out to begin restructuring his life. He spent a long period of time in the desert. He was becoming acquainted with Jesus; he was learning to know himself as Jesus knew him. He was beginning to see the world through the eyes of its Maker. He was allowing the Holy Spirit to pour God's love into his heart.

Occasionally I hear of someone today who takes the time to restructure his life. But many people continue at the same dogged pace, living with a sense of deep

146

dissatisfaction—pursuing money, success, or approval from others.

When the deepest needs of his life were met, Paul was willing to give up everything that had seemed so important before. His reputation as a Jew, his position of influence in Jerusalem, his aristocratic background, his superior education—all of these were no more important than manure in comparison with what he now had!

Paul had forgiveness; he had love; he had recognition; he had approval; he had a new purpose in life. All his personal needs were met as he allowed Jesus to permeate and direct his life. This was the great Spirit of the universe—all loving, all powerful, all wise—who was shaping Paul into a new person. He would soon be ready to give himself to the needs of other people.

Years later when he wrote the letter to the Christians at Rome he could say with satisfaction: "So it is all right for me to be a little proud of all Christ Jesus has done through me. I dare not judge how effectively he has used others, but I know this: he has used me to win the Gentiles to God" (Rom. 15:17-18, TLB).

But it hadn't been easy. He had endured beatings, imprisonments, shipwrecks, and all types of danger and persecution. He had survived hunger, thirst, and exposure to the cold. He had traveled constantly and worked tirelessly. He had known daily pressure and anxiety for the churches. (See 2 Cor. 11:22-23.)

Most people would have given up in frustration or in anger. How could Paul continue year after year on this kind of mission? Wasn't there a more enjoyable way to live?

The answer is that his needs were being met by the Holy Spirit both directly and through the people in the churches. He often told the people how much he loved them and how much their love meant to him. He was not on his mission merely out of duty or obligation. He had a deep conviction that this was what he was meant to do. He was helping to change the course of history.

Paul's plans were always expanding. He wanted to visit the Christians at Rome. He wanted to carry the gospel west into Spain. More adventure, new experiences, great satisfaction—preaching the gospel in a country where it never had been preached before. These were big plans. Paul was eager to go. But first there was business at home to be taken care of.

His assignment included more than winning the Gentiles. It included taking care of the Christian family— those who had already been won. The Jewish Christians in Jerusalem were going through particular hardships. Many of them were painfully poor. The Gentile churches in Greece and Macedonia were willing to help them. Paul hoped this gesture of love from Gentile churches to Jewish Christians would help do away with the feelings of prejudice that many Christians were still harboring. Paul longed to see this prejudice disappear from the church so that all Christians could truly be one.

He was concerned for the poor in Jerusalem, and he was concerned for the unity of the church. A committee could take the gift of money to Jerusalem, but Paul felt compelled to go along himself—even though it would be quite dangerous for him to show up in Jerusalem. The Jewish officials had not forgiven him for converting to Christianity and especially for trying to convince Jews everywhere to do the same. Their goal was to get rid of Paul.

After Paul had taken care of this "family" matter, arduous and dangerous as the trip would be, he then would feel free to answer the call to Spain and visit the Romans en route.

In Romans 15 Paul was explaining all this: "For I am planning to take a trip to Spain, and when I do, I will stop off there in Rome; and after we have had a good time together for a little while, you can send me on my way again.

"But before I come, I must go down to Jerusalem to take a gift to the Jewish Christians there. For you see, the Christians in Macedonia and Achaia have taken up an offering for those in Jerusalem who are going through such hard times. They were very glad to do this, for they feel that they owe a real debt to the Jerusalem Christians . . . . As soon as I have delivered this money and completed this good deed of theirs, I will come to see you on my way to Spain. And I am sure that when I come the Lord will give me a great blessing for you" (vv. 24-27,28-32, TLB).

There is an important lesson here for all of us: Make exciting plans for the future, but don't neglect the present needs. God seldom wants us to go galloping off on some adventure for him when there is unfinished business at home.

We have a Christian responsibility to disciple other people, but it begins first with ourselves and with our own families. Too many Christian parents fail their own children. There is not enough attention at home—not enough understanding, not enough guidance. There is not enough listening to one another.

How about communications within your own family? Are there wide rifts and hurt feelings? Are you willing to take on the arduous, risky, and time-consuming business of learning to relate lovingly and intimately to your own family members?

Have you allowed God to satisfy *your* spiritual hunger? Have you allowed him to point out areas of need in your own life and in your family's? Make it a priority to deal with resentment, frustration, feelings of inferiority, fear, pride, worry, anger. Some people know the difficulty involved in truly taking care of themselves and their families. They avoid it *religiously.* Ministry begins at home—to the person within you, to the persons around you. Only then are you ready to reach out to distant people and to those you haven't met.

Paul had claimed God's peace for himself. He was doing what he could to bring peace within the Christian family. Having done these first things, he would be free to get on with his long-range mission: sharing the gospel of Christ. That's what he was doing here; that was the goal of his life.

Someone has said, "How can I exist unless I have a purpose?" We all feel the necessity of having a mission in life. Some people find their true mission in ministering to their own families and their larger church family. Other people feel restless until they are confronted with a larger purpose. It has to do with putting their dominant talent or ability to good use. Or it has to do with Erikson's principle of deciding "what or whom you can take care of."

There are many worthwhile causes in this world. Countless wrongs need to be righted. Scores of world-wide responsibilities must be shouldered. God still needs people who are willing to help change the course of history. The kingdom of God needs to come to many lives in unheard-of places. There's a mission in life for you—either close at hand or far away.

In the conclusion of his letter to the Romans, Paul sends personal greetings to the families and individuals in Rome whom he has known in the past or known of (chap. 16). He urges the Roman Christians to pray fervantly about his dangerous visit to Jerusalem (15:30-31). He prays that they will know joy and peace, hope and power in their lives (15:13).

Scholars tell us that Paul apparently never made it to Spain. He lost his freedom as the result of his trip to Jerusalem. But he did finally make it to Rome—as a prisoner of the Roman government. He was allowed to live in a guarded house in Rome and was able for some time to carry on his ministry there. We know from his prison letters that even prison did not curb his joy and his sense of mission. His ministry continued through the letters he wrote and through his personal contacts with Christians and non-Christians. Near the end of his life he could say, "I have fought the good fight, I have finished the race, I have kept the faith" (2 Tim. 4:7).

You can do the same. See that your own spiritual and emotional needs are taken care of. Take care of the needs in your own home. Make yourself available to God. Find your mission in life.

"May God, the source of hope, fill you with all joy and peace . . . so that you will continue to grow by the power of the Holy Spirit" (Rom. 15:13, RSV).

God sees a beautiful you!

To Think About and Do:

1. Consider the needs in your own family. Do you spend enough time together as a family? It's a good idea to set aside at least one night or one afternoon a week for playing together and listening to one another.

2. Consider buying *The Ungame* (The Ungame Co., Anaheim, California, 92806) to improve communication in your family. Two to six people can play, and it is designed to encourage sharing and listening and the exploration of attitudes, feelings, motives, and values.

3. What are you doing to promote spiritual growth in your family? Does it include activities at home as well as those at church?

4. Does your schedule include blocks of time for you to spend alone? These times can be spent for your own spiritual growth and for considering the values, motives, and goals of your life.

5. Become better acquainted with needs in your own city or county (hunger, poverty, discrimination, delinquency, drug and alcohol addiction, mental health, environmental concerns). How can you help? Do these qualify for "Christian mission"? Is one of these the answer to "what or whom you can take of"?

6. Jesus ministered to both the spiritual and physical needs of people. Are you concerned about needy people in other parts of the world? How can you become involved?

7. God still needs people to help change the course of history. Are you available?